HOW TO THINK
THEOLOGICALLY

Second Edition

Howard W. STONE
James O. DUKE

FORTRESS PRESS
MINNEAPOLIS

HOW TO THINK THEOLOGICALLY
Second Edition

Cover image: Image Source / Getty Images. Used by permission.
Cover and book design: James Korsmo

Further materials for study of this volume are available at fortresspress
.com.

Library of Congress Cataloging-in-Publication Data

Stone, Howard W.
  How to think theologically / Howard W. Stone and James O. Duke.—
Rev. ed.
      p. cm.
  Includes bibliographical references and index.
  ISBN 0-8006-3818-2 (alk. paper)
  1. Theology—Methodology. I. Duke, James O. II. Title.
BR118.S75 2006
230.01—dc22
                                    2005033729

Manufactured in the U.S.A.

10   09   08   07   06   1   2   3   4   5   6   7   8   9   10

CONTENTS

For KAREN and JEANNE

PREFACE
TO THE SECOND EDITION

AS IT TURNS OUT, WE WERE NOT THE ONLY PERSONS who wondered about how you go about thinking theologically. In fact, we have been overwhelmed by the response to the first edition of *How to Think Theologically*. We have heard from students in Ph.D. seminars, others in the first year in seminary, and many in local churches who are interested in reflecting more seriously on their faith. The breadth of interest and the number of you who have used the book is exciting. We want to thank all of our past readers and welcome those who are new to doing theological reflection— or at least new to our book.

The good response to *How to Think Theologically* allows us to do a revised edition. What? you may say. Has the way people think theologically changed in the last ten years? Not really—but the way we relate our faith to the world around us is always in flux because the world is constantly changing. Preparing a revised edition gives us an opportunity to make some changes and include some things we left out in the first edition, including updates to some of the case studies. We want to thank the many people who shared with us their comments and questions, thereby helping to make the book better and more comprehensive.

What is different about this edition? First, we have added a chapter; there was more we wanted to say in chapter 8 so we split it into two (the old chapter 8 is now chapters 8 and 9) and added to each. Second, because a number of you asked what you should read next we have added a section entitled "For Further Reading" to assist in those choices. Third, we have made some changes to the discussions of the three diagnostic exercises in chapters 5 through 7. Your comments helped us realize that there were some things we did not say in the first-edition versions that needed to be included in this revision. Fourth, we have updated the bibliographic references in the notes. Fifth, we have rewritten and updated several of the case studies. And finally, we have expanded and made some changes to the glossary at the end of the book.

Never has sound theological reflection on the part of Christians been more necessary than in this post-9/11 era. When a quarter of a million people die in a single natural disaster (as witnessed in the tsunami that hit Southeast Asia in late 2004), three million people in Africa die each year from AIDS, millions more groan with rampant hunger and poverty, and war continues to tear the world apart, we must bring our faith to bear upon the small and big decisions we make each day. How we think theologically does make a difference. It is a way we witness to our faith.

All Christians are theologians. We make that point repeatedly in the book. *How to Think Theologically* suggests a process by which Christians can relate their faith to everyday experience. It proposes a way to go about this everyday task so that the outcome of our theological thinking is less tangled and more careful.

We would like to thank a number of people for their assistance with this book: our wives Karen and Jeanne for urging us to write the book in the first place; Brite Divinity School, Texas Christian University, for the place to teach and the opportunity to continue to test our ideas about thinking theologically; Michael West, our editor at Fortress for his encouragement and assistance throughout the writing of both of these editions of the book; and finally, all the Christians in churches, colleges, seminaries who are daily thinking about theology. Thanks again for your kind comments that have made this revised edition of *How to Think Theologically* possible. Keep those cards and letters (and e-mails) coming.

We are especially grateful to the Rev. Ben G. Hubert, Senior Minister of First Christian Church in San Angelo, Texas. He has graciously and helpfully composed a thoughtful study guide to *How To Think Theologically*. Readers in college, seminary, or congregational settings will benefit from Ben's intelligent illuminations of the book's key concepts and sections. We invite readers to consult Ben's study guide at fortresspress.com.

PREFACE
TO THE FIRST EDITION

SOME OF OUR COLLEAGUES MAY THINK THAT ALL WE do is drink coffee or go out to eat. Our first collaboration, *The Caring Christian,* began at a coffee break. The origins of the present book can be traced to a hole-in-the-wall restaurant on the south side of Fort Worth one Friday evening in 1990. The two of us with our wives were enjoying Greek food and discussing a question I (Howard) had asked Jim several weeks before: How do you teach students to reflect theologically? What process do you suggest to help them relate theology to their day-to-day experiences?

The matter sparked lively discussion among the four of us. We discussed the difficulty of thinking theologically about everyday events in the work world, in our personal lives, in our marriage and family relationships, in issues of social or public policy—even in the church.

We noted that seminary professors frequently urge students to give a theological response to various issues, such as the meaning of ordination, the purpose of the church, abortion, or world hunger. And, recalling the last faculty meeting, we began to wonder how well we professors were able to give theological responses to pressing concerns of the day. While we ask students to reflect theologically, we do not often give them explicit guidance about how to do so effectively. Quite possibly some of us do our own theological thinking in a haphazard fashion.

The discussion continued over coffee at Howard's house (the restaurant, inexplicably, was out of coffee!). Jeanne (Jim's wife), who is herself a seminary graduate, said, "The two of you have already worked together; why don't you write a book on this topic?" Karen (Howard's wife), who has written on the subject of methods for interpreting art, joined in. We both laughed and changed the subject. Both wives made the suggestion again. Finally, we began to take the idea seriously. After a period of germination, the result is before you.

How to Think Theologically begins with the premise that all Christians are theologians, simply because they are Christian. The question is not whether or not you are a theologian—you are!—but how adequate the resulting theological reflection is in light of the Christian faith.

This book does not present a systematic theology or propose a one-and-only-one way of doing theology. It offers, instead, a framework in which to do ongoing theological reflection. Our hope is that you, the reader, will gain confidence to go about thinking theologically on your own. The suggestions we make are to help you think theologically in real-life situations as well as aid your efforts in responding to other theologians. Adapt them to your own heritage, situation, and experience. A responsible theologian is informed by circumstances and events but not pushed around by them. A responsible theologian is guided by deliberations on the historic themes of faith, by scripture and tradition, by worship, and by engaged service in the world.

The suggestions we offer are linked by two common techniques: *listening* and *questioning.* Listening involves an active waiting that allows new information in, is prepared to be surprised, remains open to the illumination of the Spirit. Questioning is a corrective to complacency—the danger of becoming satisfied with old answers and preconceptions. We subject our own answers of yesterday to fresh questioning in order to embrace new situations and new insights. The aim of listening is receptivity; the aim of questioning is honesty. All of the aids for theological reflection discussed in this book are to be applied with this back-and-forth movement between listening and questioning. The ultimate goal of the process is the maturing of our theological understanding. We listen and question and at last bring things together, fashioning conclusions that we set forth in our statements of belief and realize in our actions. These conclusions are important decisions of faith. They are in a true sense firmly held. Yet in another, equally true sense they always remain tentative, ready for retesting as our journey in faith continues. The cycle of reflection is continually in motion. We probe and wait, ask and receive, decide and act.

We would like to thank a number of individuals for helping to shape and refine this volume. First, Karen and Jeanne must be thanked; if it were not for their urging, the book would not have come into being. They not only made the suggestion but read and offered criticism for various drafts. In addition, we would like to thank Robert Benne, Don Browning, Sue Hamly, and Stephen Sprinkle for taking time from their busy schedules to read the manuscript and offer suggestions. We would also like to thank Shirley Bubar for help in the preparation of the manuscript. Working collaboratively has its perils, not least of which is the difficulty of bringing together two styles and points of view. (In this regard we may be forgiven for comparing theologians to snowflakes; however much we may agree, no two of us is ever alike.) We owe much to the extended collaboration of these readers in helping us to speak clearly and with one voice.

INTRODUCTION

CHANCES ARE, YOU ARE A THEOLOGIAN.

If you practice your religion, live according to your Christian faith, or even take seriously the spiritual dimension of life, inescapably you think theologically.

It is a simple fact of life for Christians: their faith makes them theologians. Deliberately or not, they think—and act—out of a theological understanding of existence, and their faith calls them to become the best theologians they can be.

Not me, you may say. I believe what I've been taught, but I am not equipped for theological thinking. Maybe I'm not even very interested in it—to me theology is a subject for academics, philosophers, professors, Ph.D.s.

Such a response is understandable. Theology is widely taken to be a field for experts alone, too arcane for the day-to-day concerns of ordinary parishioners and their ministers. This impression is due in part to their off-putting encounters with the writings and speeches of theologians. "If this is theology," they say, "it's not for me."

Put that way, the point is so honest and so fitting that we would not argue against it even if we could. Even so, we hold to a time-honored conviction that when Christians are baptized they enter into a ministry they all share, responding to a God-given call to disclose the gospel (God's good news of Jesus Christ) through all they say and do. Their calling makes them witnesses of faith, and hence theologians as well. This is because the witness they make in the course of their daily lives sets forth their implicit understanding of the meaning of the Christian faith, and—in keeping with another time-honored conviction—because Christian theology is at its root a matter of faith seeking understanding.

Every aspect of the life of the church and its members is a theological testimony. So too are the particular ways Christians have of relating to what is around them, their styles of interacting

| To be Christian at all is to be a theologian. There are no exceptions. |

with others and the world. Even if they were to run off and live in some remote Canadian forest (and there are days for many of us when such a prospect sounds inviting!), that decision would itself be a theological one. Likewise, choices they make about their wilderness lifestyle—how to live among the trees, the lakes, and the animals—would signal something of their understanding of God's creation. *To be Christian at all is to be a theologian. There are no exceptions.*

Our faith is at once a gift of God and a human response; theology is an integral part of that human response. Theology is a seeking after understanding—a process of thinking about life in the light of the faith that Christians engage in because of their calling. In this book we invite Christians to give some thought to the doing of this theology. Chapters 1 through 3 present a sketch of how and why Christians do theology, what is happening when they do it, and where they turn for knowledge and support. Chapters 4 through 7 discuss theological method and present three diagnostic exercises for those whose faith leads them to press on with the tasks of theology. Chapter 8 speaks of theology as a critical inquiry in community. Chapter 9 addresses spiritual disciplines that undergird our entire theological enterprise.

We will focus on the process of thinking theologically, calling it by one of its best-known names—*theological reflection*. We will suggest, as theologians often do, that theological reflection is a process in many respects like a craft;[1] it involves working with various materials or resources, applying certain skills which can be learned and honed over time by concentration and practice. Since we are convinced that all Christians are theologians, our aim is only to help speed them along their way.

We are hopeful that laypeople and seminarians will find here an orientation to theological reflection that can be put to use right away and built upon over time. We will point out some of the most common issues and terms of theological writing and describe a direct method for working with theology. Ordained ministers, who in all likelihood have already had some theological training, may find here a refresher course with a number of suggestions and words of encouragement for their ongoing work in theology.

Our focus on the *doing* of theology distinguishes this book from most textbook introductions to theology, or from popular accounts of theology, which are readily available. These works usually survey the basics of Christian doctrine, major figures and movements of the past, or present-day issues and trends. The approach we take does not replace such resources. There is no substitute for the study of accomplished theologians, even though the reading can be tough going. What is more, taking in the performance of a theological superstar does not necessarily enable the reader to go and do likewise. Starting off with the end result can make the process seem more intimidating and less manageable than it actually is.

That said, we admit that introducing theology in this way is not without its intimidating or unmanageable aspects. At least a few disclaimers are in order. First, we do not tell all that is to be told, or even all that we would have to tell if we were to write a longer, more detailed book on the topic. Plus, what we have to say comes with emphases and accents very much our own. Thus, for example, although theological reflection takes place in philosophy and every world religion, our references to it (and to theology and theologians) are limited to the Christian sphere unless otherwise noted. Within this sphere we give center stage to church theology—the theological reflection where Christians consider faith, church ministry, and the Christian life. And, although we have tried to describe how Christian theology is done in very general, flexible, and nonpartisan terms, the language we use is certainly not all-encompassing or altogether neutral. We assume—as we believe theologians always should—that our remarks can be expanded, contested, corrected, and even censured by others whose backgrounds and theologies are different from our own. And no, although we speak in accord on these pages, the two of us do not agree on every point of theology.

THEOLOGICAL REFLECTION

Since theological reflection can be a demanding task, theologians often go off to work alone in peace and quiet. Scholars work in the library, pastors in their studies. Churches hold retreats where their members can contemplate and discuss their faith away from the hubbub of daily life. Christians rise early or stay up late to make times for themselves to read Scripture, pray, and meditate on the Word.

But serious thinking about the meaning of Christian faith can and does take place anywhere. It goes on while conversing, worshiping, weathering a life crisis, keeping up with the latest news, working, taking some time out for recreation. Wherever and whenever it occurs, theological reflection is not only a personal but also an interactive, dialogical, and community-related process. The voices of others are heard. Some of these voices, like those of the biblical writers, come from texts of centuries past. Others are those of our contemporaries. Still others are our own. These voices offer us

> Wherever and whenever it occurs, theological reflection is not only a personal but also an interactive, dialogical, and community-related process.

food for thought, to be heeded or debated or improved upon or set aside as unhelpful.

To engage in theological reflection is to join in an ongoing conversation with others that began long before we ever came along and will continue long after we have passed away. Realizing that theology is a perpetual conversation is something of a comfort to most theologians. It is not up to you or me or anyone else to invent Christian theology, to control it, or even to perfect it. We are called only to do the best we can, given who and where we are. This is actually the best that theologians ever manage, not only because as humans they are limited and fallible and because times change, but because the final word is God's alone. Until that final word is spoken, each and every Christian has a contribution to make to the conversation—a duty to listen, and a question to ask.

This is not to say, however, that being conversational makes theology easy or pleasant. Conversations do not always go well. They are sometimes bitter, pointless, mean-spirited, painful, or futile. Accounts of strife within certain Christian denominations regularly make the evening news.

Nor are all those with something to contribute to the conversation given a hearing. The voices of the vast majority of Christians throughout history have had no hearing outside their immediate and very limited sphere. Their theological contributions are out of sight, out of mind, difficult if not impossible to recover, except as they have affected the spiritual lives of those people close to them, perhaps their children and their children's children through an oral tradition.

The significance of that effect, of course, should not be underestimated. One friend of ours tells of the importance her grandmother's theology played in her own understandings of the faith. Her grandmother, recipient of an oral theological tradition from her own parents and grandparents, interpreted her own experience in light of that theology and time and passed it on to her children. The core theological interpretation of all her experience—that God always was and always would be with her, no matter what—she expressed in the words and deeds of her daily life, and confidently verbalized on her deathbed: "Underneath are the everlasting arms." That conviction of God's abiding presence became a key feature of her children's life of faith, and of her grandchildren's. Who can predict how long it will continue to be felt?

Countless Christians find cause to believe that theology is a conversation that is closed or stacked against them. The Third World, African American, and feminist or womanist theologies of our times are foremost among those that offer exposés of this failing as well as correctives to it. To them can be added the biblical, historical, and contemporary studies that seek to uncover the life and work of people other than the famous church leaders and scholars of Christian history. No theologian can know about everyone and everything. To learn more than we already know is one good reason to enter into conversation with others. Limiting the circle of conversation partners in advance, whether due to prejudice or ignorance, is always the theologian's loss. That makes it the church's loss as well.

Viewing theological reflection as an extended conversation may help put into proper perspective the roles that individuality and commonality play in the process. A Christian's theology is, of course, very much his or her own. It witnesses to the Christian faith as the theologian has come to understand it. Yet a theology is never the theologian's—yours or mine—alone. Inasmuch as it claims to be Christian, it aspires to a status that cannot be granted by any one person's say-so. The Christian faith it purports to understand is personal but not private. It is a faith shared by others. A lively exchange of views among the varied members of the body is essential for the church's theological well-being. Christians carry out, in this way, their ministry of mutual concern, mutual accountability, and mutual instruction. Each member's contribution may serve to enliven and enrich the conversation as a whole.

In case this sounds like too rosy a picture, we cannot forget that disagreements over the meaning of the common Christian faith have also led to division. Some of these divisions, in hindsight, have proven to be regrettable. Instead of bringing people together, theological reflection has at times highlighted differences.

A model of theological reflection based on conversation allows for an appreciation of diversity, healthy debate, and creative tension. It does not, however, gloss over the difficulties of coping with divergent theologies or endorse an "anything goes" policy. At certain points Christians must set limits. There are things said and done in the name of Christianity to which we must respond—because of our understanding of the faith—with a firm no. "Here I stand," we must say, or "This theology is a profound misunderstanding of faith and cannot be condoned." In such cases, the model of theological reflection outlined here is still valuable. It reminds us of a crucial question to be addressed before making this (or any other) theological judgment: Have we given the point at issue careful, thorough, dialogical, deliberative consideration? When we have, then we must say yes or no and act upon it.

The work of theology is a matter of personalized conversational thinking about shared convictions. It routinely deals with common topics, grapples with common issues, visits and revisits many common themes, and draws upon a common stock of tools and materials. Such points of connection invite other Christians to identify and acknowledge the "Christianness" of the work. In sum, theological reflection is bound up with a vast and yet intimately

> A model of theological reflection based on conversation allows for an appreciation of diversity, healthy debate, and creative tension.

related community of faith called the church. Its aim is less to set forth *my* understanding of my Christian faith than to develop the best possible understanding of the faith that our Christian church seeks to understand.

FAITH SEEKING UNDERSTANDING

Christians would surely feel more comfortable about their calling as theologians if they knew exactly what they had gotten themselves into. Unfortunately, there is no universally accepted definition of the term *theology*. It comes to us as a compound word from ancient Greek: *theo-logia* are *logia* (sayings, accounts, teachings, theories) concerning *theos* (the divine, gods and goddesses, God). This root meaning carries over into the most traditional use of the word: a belief, conception, or study of God. It is unusual, however, to limit theology to its strictest sense. Two extended uses of the term are commonplace.

First, *theology* is typically expanded to embrace the totality of things having to do with religious life. Not only ideas of God per se, but everything associated with faith, church, and ministry, are said to be theological. This expansion comes about quite naturally, because Christian belief in God neither arose nor exists in splendid isolation. It is the focal point of the life of faith as a whole. In keeping with its Jewish origins, early Christianity centered itself on a conviction about the arrival of a message from God. Various terms, such as the Word of God, the *kerygma* (proclamation), and the Way, were used to designate God's self-disclosure. Among the earliest and most prominent terms for the subject matter of this message was *gospel*, God's good news to the world. The gospel has to do with the salvation that God brought about through Jesus of Nazareth, the Christ. Contemporary theologians refer to this core of faith in a wide variety of ways, such as divine revelation, the

Christian mythos, the Christ-event, the fundamental datum of Christianity, and so forth. What do all these terms mean? Simply this: that essential to the Christian religion is a message from God concerning God's relationship to the world, to history, and to all of human life.

Interpretations of this complex of relationships are focal points of Christian theology. The subject matter embraces the nature and will of God, the person and work of Jesus Christ, the activity of the Holy Spirit, creation, redemption, and hope. It also embraces everything connected with faith, church, ministry, and the Christian life. And so, by extension, various fields of study touching on these matters are swept into theology. The result is that theology as a whole divides and subdivides into various emphases. Modern theological education customarily groups these studies under the broad rubrics of biblical theology, historical theology, systematic theology, and practical theology. These make for a sometimes bewildering array, especially considering the plethora of other common headings, such as moral theology, sacramental theology, pastoral theology, confessional theology, theology of culture, African American theology, theology of ministry, liberation theology, and on and on.

Second, *theology* is often used in an extended sense that has to do with the function of statements about God in Christianity, and the transcendent in the other religions and societies of the world. That function is not merely to designate a divine being or beings, but to signal a commitment to what people value most highly. In this functional sense, the divine (*theos*) has to do with whatever individuals, communities, or cultures regard to be of ultimate sig-

> Christians are aware that some people's object of ultimate concern may bear little resemblance to their God, or to any deity of any religion.

nificance in their lives. For Christians this ultimate concern is God and the message of God.

Christians are aware, however, that some people's object of ultimate concern may bear little resemblance to their God, or to any deity of any religion. Money, fame, nation, or family may be treated as a god. A political or cultural movement may serve for some people as the functional alternative to the deity of historical religion. Groups devoted to great causes may turn into quasi religions, organizing their communities under the lead of apostles, prophets, teachers, and theologians of their own.

This phenomenon has long found its place in Christian awareness. Christians confess that they believe in God and in God's message of salvation in Jesus Christ. But the understanding of faith that they seek is by no means a matter of rote memorization or book learning, theory, or speculation. Belief as intellectual assent is only one component of a living faith. It is a knowing of the sort that exists in interpersonal relationships: more a knowing *of* God than a knowing *about* God, in that it involves emotion, valuing, and living in relationship.

Historically, emphasis on Christian *orthodoxy* (correct opinion or belief) has always been balanced by warnings against giving lip service to the faith while acting as if other concerns are more important than the God revealed in Jesus Christ. Faith involves believing, but it is not reducible to mere assent. Cautionary tales abound of self-professed believers whose views have no impact on the way they live: the televangelist who bilks millions from unsuspecting individuals; the Christian department head who lies to her staff rather than take responsibility for her decisions; the Christian computer software technician who professes to have grown spiritually but pads his hours, does sloppy work, and quits before the job is finished.

A frequent response to orthodoxy without active commitment is its counterpart: *orthopraxy* (correct practice) without thoughtful theological reflection. "What you do is more important than what you say" is heard from the adherents of orthopraxy. This response is often wholesome, and at times altogether necessary. A distinction between belief and practice, however, can only be pressed so far. There is a belief component in orthopraxy, for it involves not only a belief that God wills us to act in a certain way rather than some other way but also a belief that how we act is more telling than what we say we believe. Emphasis on orthopraxy has always been modified by warnings against merely going through motions that appear truly Christian while covertly, in our heart of hearts, devoting ourselves to someone other than God and something other than God's message.

The Christian message of God calls for both beliefs and actions. It also elicits an emotional response of love, trust, and dedication. Thus the word *faith* is often used, as we will use it here, as a comprehensive term for all elements of the Christian life: belief, action, and heartfelt devotion to God as the object of ultimate concern in a living faith. All three need to be considered in any understanding of that faith—that is, in theology.

To say that theology is "faith seeking understanding" is to say this: that as theologians we seek to understand what we believe about the Christian message of God, and how we as individuals and as a community are to live in light of that message.

CHAPTER 1

FAITH, UNDERSTANDING, AND REFLECTION

MURIEL WAS A PROFESSOR OF ART (NOW RETIRED) AT a major university. She used to leave her office door unlocked so students and colleagues could walk in and leave messages on her mural-sized bulletin board, a collage of clippings, photographs, sketches, and notes. For about a year, two items stood out from the creative clutter. One was a large, carefully lettered card left by an anonymous visitor: *Muriel, everything is really very simple.* Just below it a subsequent (also anonymous) caller had tacked a sheet of notebook paper on which he or she had scrawled in black marker: *Muriel, nothing is ever simple.*

Whenever you ask an expert how to do an unfamiliar task, watch out if the person responds, "It's simple! You just . . ." It isn't going to be simple.

A simple-sounding definition of theological reflection is "faith seeking understanding." It is a promising staging area from which to start out upon theological reflection. The journey, of course, will not be as uncomplicated as the phrase might imply (*Muriel, nothing is ever simple*). Each of us does theology at different levels and in different ways. Theology is simple. Theology is complex.

To become aware of having any faith at all is to have some idea of its meaning. Christian faith, therefore, carries with it a measure of understanding at the outset. This understanding of faith's meaning develops within us in much the same way as a language is learned. From what the church says and does, from contact and involvement with others, we first come to understand ourselves as Christian.

But that word *Christian* is itself a highly charged label, and giving an account of its meaning is one of the perennial tasks of theology. Based on what most of the churches have said about it most of the time, we gather that Christian identity has to do with faith in God, Jesus Christ, and the Holy Spirit, with the gospel, with

> What people understand their Christian faith to mean varies from one age to another, from denomination to denomination, from congregation to congregation, and from person to person.

taking part in the life and ministry of the church, with upholding certain ethical principles and ideals, and so on. To say only this much about the meaning of Christian faith, however, is to operate at a broad and abstract level. It leaves us far from either the specific or the full meaning that the faith holds for Christians. Pressing on, we note that what people understand their Christian faith to mean varies from one age to another, from denomination to denomination, from congregation to congregation, and from person to person.

Here is an example of the difficulty. Not so long ago, a debate took place in Texas Christian University's student newspaper on the subject of the school's alcohol policy. Letters to the editor argued that if TCU were really "Christian," alcohol would be banned on campus. To this, other writers responded that a Christian school ought to respect the right of each student to decide whether or not to drink a beer. Both groups of writers seemed to assume that once they had explained what being a Christian university meant, university officials would act accordingly. It is impossible to gauge how ultimate a concern this was to the debaters, but in stating their understandings of what Christianity means in one particular instance, they were (perhaps unwittingly) acting as theologians. The controversy stemmed from differing understandings of faith—that is, differing theologies.

In the debate on drinking, differing theologies are at odds, and because of these differences, neither view can be taken for granted. Theology is both a given and a continuing task. Such debates, especially when their topics may appear to be of far greater consequence than this example, remind us that for Christians understanding what the faith means is both a given and a continuing task. There are initial understandings that we have more or less grown into and that we take for granted. And there are efforts to seek increased understanding. The following comments will look at the theological interplay of our faith: our initial or implicit understandings and our quest for greater understanding.

EMBEDDED THEOLOGY

Christians learn what faith is all about from countless daily encounters with their Christianity—formal and informal, planned and unplanned. This understanding of faith, disseminated by the church and assimilated by its members in their daily lives, will be called *embedded theology*. The phrase points to the theology that is deeply in place and at work as we live as Christians in our homes, churches, and the world. Other terms would surely work as well. In religious language, what we are calling embedded theology is often known as *first-order theology* or *the language of witness*, being made up of the most immediate and direct testimonies to the meaning of faith. It is rooted (embedded) in the preaching and practices of the

Christians learn what faith is all about from countless daily encounters with their Christianity—formal and informal, planned and unplanned.

church and its members. It is the implicit theology that Christians live out in their daily lives.

Every church community sees itself to be conducting its affairs in accord with Christian faith. What it says and does is intended to fulfill the church's mission of bearing witness to God's gospel in Jesus Christ and instrumenting God's will in the world. Its words and deeds reflect what these Christians understand to be called for by their faith. How well they may have thought about or studied the Christian message is in one sense beside the point. Testimony of this sort is the outcome of theological reflection, and the messages arising from such theological reflection comprise embedded theology. The theological messages intrinsic in and communicated by praying, preaching, hymn singing, personal conduct, liturgy, social action or inaction, and virtually everything else people say and do in the name of their Christian faith fall into this category.

The meaning of Christian faithfulness is conveyed in many and varied ways. It is communicated by *teaching and learning the language of faith*—a symbolic language, inasmuch as it deals in images, metaphors, analogies, and stories whose plain meanings serve to point beyond themselves to other matters relating to God, faith, and spiritual life. The role that the language of faith plays in passing on an embedded theology can hardly be overestimated.

Christian practices also communicate the meaning of Christian faith. Children learn, for example, that being Christian means going to church for worship and knowing how to behave there— when to stand, sit, or kneel, and when to listen, pray, or sing. From words and action together comes familiarity with an entire set of meanings associated with the faith: good and bad; rituals and customs; and organizations, programs, and activities. Theological understandings are embedded in these actions, no less than in the grammar and vocabulary of the language of faith.

These theological messages from the church have been bred into the hearts and minds of the faithful since our entry into the church. Many of us were born and raised in this theology. It began in us before we could speak, developed during years of Sunday worship, church school, and youth groups, and was reinforced by the life example of our parents, friends, and ministers. As we grew older and began to think for ourselves, this theology was reshaped and became very much our own, in some ways like and in other respects unlike the theology we encountered in our homes and churches. The development may have unfolded as a slow, steady, trouble-free growth; or it may have been stormy, as we questioned or even rejected our childhood understanding of faith in favor of another understanding.

Some of us find it easy to articulate the embedded theology that we carry with us. But many do not. Ask any of us: What is your concept of God, your understanding of sin or salvation, your

> We make decisions at work and play, in our families and in society, according to our embedded understanding of God's message.

account of the nature and purpose of the church, or your Christian view of right and wrong? Caught short by the question, we may come up with a pat answer. Or we may hesitate and stammer, unless we have stopped at some earlier point to consider the matter. And yet our day-to-day decisions are based upon this embedded theology. We pray to the God of this theology. This is the God we love or fear—and serve and sin against. We make decisions at work and play, in our families and in society, according to our embedded understanding of God's message.

Embedded theology is what devoted Christians have in mind when they say things like "My faith and my church mean a lot to me." Wrapped up in such simple statements is a host of associated elements—memories, beliefs, feelings, values, and hopes—not necessarily stated, and perhaps not at all clear.

Embedded theology is also the stuff that makes for a great deal of real-world skepticism and indifference. It is unlikely that many people shy away from Christianity because they have thoroughly examined all the arguments and conclude that its claims are not intellectually compelling. More probably, they give up on the faith because of what they have gathered about it from the embedded theological testimonies or actions of other people and their churches. Most mental health professionals and pastoral counselors have spent time tending counselees who were scarred by what passed for Christianity in their homes or their home churches.

And it is embedded theology that rushes to the front line in every battle over the moral and social issues of the day. Christians rise up to defend their theological convictions or express outrage

> Whether or not church people understand the meaning of Christian faith adequately and communicate it effectively makes a real-world difference.

when those convictions are threatened. Turn on the evening news and witness the two sides of the abortion question facing off: even their placards testify to their differing embedded understandings of faith.

No wonder, then, that so many Christian laity and clergy alike often report that they feel as though they are living in the trenches. They are! They volunteer or are pressed by others to enter the fray, taking their stands on one side or another of the great debates of the day. To take time to weigh theological options is to risk being tagged a know-nothing or do-nothing Christian. If it is any comfort, it has always been so. Whether or not church people understand the meaning of Christian faith adequately and communicate it effectively makes a real-world difference. The professional, academically credentialed theologians of the church are expected to lend some support and guidance; after all, they have special expertise. But the final burden rests with ordinary Christians—parishioners and pastors—who face daily opportunities and conflicts with whatever resources their embedded theologies provide them.

Life in the trenches is exciting and challenging, and sometimes ugly. The theology we operate with cannot be tied up in a neat bow, as it sometimes appears to be in the published works of professional theologians. For ordained ministers and laypersons alike time is short, jobs wait to be done, emergencies come without a moment's notice. This is part of what the Christian life is all about, and this is the world in which Christians carry out their calling as theologians.

DELIBERATIVE THEOLOGY

Our embedded theology may seem so natural and feel so comfortable that we carry it within us for years, unquestioned and perhaps even unspoken except when we join in the words of others at worship. We may be secure in the conviction that this is what Christianity is all about and leave it at that. Indeed, laypeople are tempted to let their pastors take care of theological reflection, and pastors in turn to let the church hierarchs or scholars handle it. But occasions arise that require us to think about our embedded theology, to put it into words, and then subject it to serious second thought. Frequently, it is during crises that people first experience this call to theological reflection.

Deliberative theology is the understanding of faith that emerges from a process of carefully reflecting upon embedded theological convictions. This sort of reflection is sometimes called *second-order theology*, in that it follows upon and looks back over the implicit understandings embedded in the life of faith. By its very nature, second-order reflection is marked by a certain critical distance toward each testimony of faith. Deliberations are undertaken at a far vista, removed from the more intensely personal viewpoint of embedded theology. Feelings, memories, and (to whatever degree possible) preconceptions are either set aside or evaluated along with other pertinent data, for the purpose of discovering insights that our narrower personal view might not allow.

Deliberative reflection questions what had been taken for granted. It inspects a range of alternative understandings in search of that which is most satisfactory and seeks to formulate the meaning of faith as clearly and coherently as possible. The theologian wants to take all the testimony and evidence under advisement, press beneath the surface to the heart of the matter, and develop

> Deliberative reflection questions what had been taken for granted. It inspects a range of alternative understandings in search of that which is most satisfactory and seeks to formulate the meaning of faith as clearly and coherently as possible.

an understanding of the issue that seems capable—at least for the present—of withstanding any further appeal. This is deliberative theological thinking.

For example: A toddler wanders too near the edge of his grandparents' swimming pool, falls into the water, and drowns. The family's tortured outbursts—"Why did God allow my child to die? Why couldn't God let me die instead?"—express the issue of *theodicy,* or the problem of evil and misfortune coexisting with a God who is all-powerful and altogether good. Their embedded theology leads them to state their anguish in such terms. But their "Why?" indicates that at this very moment they face a question of faith for which their embedded theology had not fully prepared them. They are in desperate need of comfort, to be sure; friends may try to console them with the thought that their faith will pull them through. But they also desperately need to *understand.* This life crisis is also a theological crisis; real death cannot be processed in bromides or vague abstractions.

When such a crisis abates, some may put behind them the issue that stemmed from that crisis. But many others will want to pursue it. In so doing, they are led to give serious second thoughts to their initial understanding of the faith and so enter into the realm of deliberative theology.

Due to its critical distance and elevated, if not high-blown, language, some laity and even some ministers complain that deliberative theology is merely academic (or worse, unbelieving). "Will it preach?" is an oft-repeated challenge thrown by some parish pastors at the feet of professional theologians. A seriocomic cartoon gleefully circulated by several generations of seminary students portrays Jesus sitting in a pew among the congregation, sound asleep, while the preacher spouts multisyllabic theological gibberish from the pulpit. What the cartoon preacher spouts is, to some (or, we fear, many) people, deliberative theology.

The arrow is often painfully on target. Just because a theological tome is difficult to read and loaded with footnotes does not mean it is necessarily good deliberative theology. In fact, it may be lousy theology, and poor prose as well. Deliberative theology does not have to be inaccessible in order to be good, and readers of theology need not be impressed or intimidated by theologians who are only acting like they are profound.

Unfortunately, many people have shied away from deliberative theological reflection, in spite of the church's historic efforts

> Deliberative theological reflection carries us forward when our embedded theology proves inadequate.

to support theological schools where teacher-scholars engage in such reflection and seek to foster it among their students. Regrettably so, because deliberative theological reflection has a vital role to play. It serves, among other things, to keep the church honest. Its task is to be faithful to the gospel in each new age.

Deliberative theological reflection also carries us forward when our embedded theology proves inadequate. Sincere or not, our embedded theology may be ill-informed or even mistaken, sufficient only until a crisis, a conversation, a controversy, or our own spiritual growth leads us to reflect again. For some, such as those who wrestle with the question of theodicy because of a tragic death, a more deliberative view than their embedded theology offers may well be the "faith seeking understanding" that pulls them through.

But theological reflection is not only for those in crisis or for the incurably curious. An impulse within faith itself calls forth deliberative theological reflection. This impulse is *conscientiousness*. The impulse wells up within us from feeling-levels of faith so deep that words to describe it are difficult to find. It is an awareness that is at once a "fear of God" and a "joy in the Lord." Though its origins are hidden in the depths of faith, the impulse makes itself known as an intense concern to say and do only that which honors the One Holy God. Thus, conscientiousness means taking care to live lives that witness to God in the most fitting way possible.

Embedded theologies certainly can be conscientious. They are, after all, directly reflective of our faith. They are our own witness to the Christian message of God as we have come to understand it. The impulse of conscientiousness prompts us to examine whether we have been diligent theologically. Conscientious Christians are aware, like Paul, that our vision of God is always imperfect and partial, a seeing in a mirror dimly. Faith's impulse of conscientiousness causes us as Christians to continue seeking a deeper understanding of what it means to be followers of the Way.

So it is that Christians feel prompted to strive for increased understanding. That impulse leads them to compare their understanding of faith with that of others, and to deliberate over its character and adequacy. Conscientious Christians are called to be firm in their convictions. They are also called to humility with regard to their understanding of faith, and therefore eager to deepen, broaden, and (if there is good reason to do so) correct that initial understanding in light of critical deliberation.

Pressing issues of church teaching and practice also lead to theological reflection. Christians simply cannot avoid making decisions, individually and corporately, about how they will carry out their calling. Although it is certainly possible for an embedded theology to be so widely accepted or deeply entrenched in a particular church that these decisions are made automatically, this is the exception more than the rule. Decision making ordinarily reckons with alternatives. It involves airing different views and evaluating them. The responsible decision-making process reviews an entire range of options, gives each a careful and fair hearing, and seeks a conclusion that is in keeping with whatever the investigation has uncovered. Here Christians are not merely expressing their convictions; they are examining the adequacy of convictions, their own and others', in order to arrive at a deeper understanding of the meaning of faith.

THE RELATIONSHIP BETWEEN EMBEDDED AND DELIBERATIVE THEOLOGY

The boundary lines between embedded and deliberative theology are at times striking, even hard-edged, separating divergent theological convictions. For example, where one group of Christians communicates the message that everything having to do with the human body and sexuality is filthy and ungodly, deliberative theological reflection discloses that such a theology is akin to that upheld by certain groups in the early church which made distinction between spirit (as good) and the body (as evil) so strict that other Christians were led to condemn their views.

More often, though, the two orders of theology overlap and the boundaries between them exist only as points along a continuum, a matter of degree. On one hand, the theologies of church leaders or scholars—based as they are on extensive research and weighing of evidence—may appear (or pretend) to be far more deliberative than they really are. Consciously or unconsciously the theologians may have been too uncritical, too reluctant to examine and weigh alternatives to their own views, to be genuinely deliberative.

On the other hand, embedded theologies are by no means always or irretrievably undeliberative. Nearly all *Christian doctrines* or teachings ("doctrine" coming from the Latin verb *docere,* to teach) set forth in the historic creeds were composed in response to controversies over conflicting embedded theologies. Hence, at least some degree of theological deliberation is preserved, and can be detected, in their formulations of the Christian message.

In any case, to say that embedded theology is comprised of the most direct and passionate testimonies reflective of Christian faith is not to say that these words and deeds are altogether thoughtless and unconsidered. Take preaching, for instance. Many a preacher comes to the sermon-preparation task fresh from the trenches— from crises, joys, personal struggles, failures, and victories. The minister's challenge is to study the meaning of faith, to deliberate theologically, and to correlate those deliberations with life experience before fixing upon what to say. The sermon may rise out of an embedded, first-order theological understanding, but it is the hard-won result of second-order theological reflection.

Laypeople do much the same in their efforts to decide what their faith means for their personal relationships, politics, work, or leisure time. How, for example, shall we speak of God? The familiar image of God as Father bears for many Christians a comforting sense of strength and care. For others, such as those who were sexually abused by their fathers, the same image may be associated with pain and anger. It may even lead them to consider their healthy resistance to abuse as somehow wrong. Deliberative theological reflection allows them to examine their implicit theology, to separate God from Daddy, and to develop an image of God that provides a more fulfilling understanding of the faith.

Christians encounter diverse views in the church as well as in wider society, and they undergo constantly changing life experi-

> To grow in faith is to deepen, extend, and perhaps revise our understanding of its meaning and to arrive at clearer means by which to state and act on our convictions.

ence. Thus, it is both natural and inevitable that they find themselves giving serious second thought to their embedded theologies at some time or another. To grow in faith is to deepen, extend, and perhaps revise our understanding of its meaning and to arrive at clearer means by which to state and act on our convictions.

THE CHALLENGE
OF THINKING THEOLOGICALLY

Widespread as deliberative theological reflection may be, it is not so commonplace that Christians—though they are theologians—inevitably leap at the slightest chance to theologize. When the time does come for them to state their theology, many Christians hardly know what to say except to echo familiar phrases.

Consider, for example, this scenario. At their pastor's request, members of the church council of First Church met to "articulate our theology of the church" in preparation for the coming fall financial campaign. Seven of the ten said that the church was "the body of Christ," the rest called it "the people of God." When it was noted that they seemed to have two views of the church, several said almost in unison, "Right—the church is both the body of Christ and the people of God." Everybody nodded yes when one person added, "Our church is open to people with different theological views."

Gently pressed to explain what these phrases meant, one member said that the church was "where we meet with Jesus," another that "the church is made of people who obey God." Efforts to press further—Do we actually meet Jesus in church? Do all church members really obey God all the time?—began to make the group anxious. The pastor tried another tack: "Why would you say that people should come to church—say, this church in particular?" One person responded that "this is where you can find really good and caring friends," another that "God loves us if we go to church and worship."

The minister was still feeling somewhat frustrated by the brief and vague statement the church council settled upon when he described the incident to colleagues at the weekly ministers' luncheon. They were eager to talk. None said (or dared to say) that the church is "where we meet Jesus," but one pastor observed that "the Christ-event occurs there in the *kerygma*," and someone else cited the Reformation view that the church is "where the Word is preached and the sacraments are administered." One suggested that it took a skilled small-group-process leader to get a church council to discuss theology. Leaving the meeting, one of the other pastors quipped, "It seems that laypeople aren't the only ones who get scared off when they're asked to articulate their theology." Revealing our own theological views of such basic Christian concepts as "church" can be extremely hard for all of us—especially when the speaking or writing of what we believe is true to our own heart and is thoughtful as well.

Both groups said a great deal, and implied still more, about topics of theology such as the church, friendship, acts of worship, obedience, whom God loves or does not love, clergy–laity relations, and seminary teaching. At least some of the people articulated a portion of their embedded theologies with honesty and seriousness of purpose. Even so, the portions were doled out in such formulaic and shorthand terms that it was hard to know what to make of them. This was raw material for deliberative theological reflection, but not the thing itself. Sound bites about body of Christ, people of God, Christ-event, *kerygma*, and group process are not yet a deliberative theology of the church.

It may be that these understandings of the church were skimpy only because discussion time was short or the assignment unclear. Certainly all involved were doing the best they could with the resources at hand. Nor is there any doubt that all were devoted to the faith and the church. It is not the quality of devotion that makes the difference in developing a clearly worked-out deliberative theology. There have been and always will be genuine saints who are unable to articulate their theology very well. By the same

> Theological reflection cannot flourish unless it is valued and practiced in the church itself.

token, there have always been award-winning, academic theologians who are anything but genuine saints.

It is unfortunate when the Christian message of God is communicated in a way that stifles the healthy impulse toward deliberative theological reflection. There are, we hope, precious few churches like the one in a recent cartoon that placed this sign on its church door: "Please leave your hats and your minds in the cloakroom before entering the sanctuary." Theological reflection cannot flourish unless it is valued and practiced in the church itself.

Left to fend for themselves, most Christians are tempted to get by as well as they can. They may do some reading, join a class at church, or seek out their minister. Others, uncertain about where to begin, may end up doing nothing at all. For their part, harried pastors may try to steal a little time to read a book or listen to tapes of a lecture with high hopes of getting some insight or enrichment from a Big-Name Theologian. But catching up or keeping up with theological scholarship often loses its appeal in the face of so many real-life demands. There are funerals to perform, classes to teach, new members to visit, and sermons to be prepared.

The result is the same for ordained ministers and laity. Attempts to do deliberative theological reflection too frequently are piecemeal and fragmented. Even if more urgent concerns do not squeeze it out altogether, it tends to sink into the all-too-predictable ruts of embedded theology. If something is to be read, let it be congenial to the position we already hold. The briefer and simpler it is, the better. The tendency is to listen only to what we already like, and close our ears to what we already dislike. Even though faith impels us to seek an increase of understanding, though we want our witness to be well informed and responsible, and though we cannot avoid deciding among a variety of options before us, we tilt toward the familiar. At that point deliberations about the meaning of faith go no further than repeating our favorite phrases and finding fault with the views of others.

Rethinking requires self-conscious effort. It means being receptive and open, but also honest and probing. It is hard work—the sort of hard work that growth in the life of the faith calls for—and it is part of our calling as Christians.

To claim or to be claimed by any Christian faith at all is automatically to join the roster of Christian theologians. With the faith comes some measure of understanding of Christianity's message of God and a responsibility to grow in our understanding of the

> To claim or to be claimed by any Christian faith at all is automatically to join the roster of Christian theologians.

faith. Engaging in deliberative theological reflection is part of our Christian calling.

Where this calling might lead if we accept it cannot be foreseen. Those who set out on its path surely hope that the journey will be pleasant and its outcome enriching. That hope is a possibility but by no means a certainty. Striving for a degree of distance from our embedded understanding of faith and subjecting it to a searching examination may prove hard and painful work. It may lead to a dark night of the soul, or to some forty days or many years in the wilderness. What had seemed so obvious as to be beyond question may not withstand a thorough theological examination; in the final analysis it may turn out to be quite uncertain, one option among many, or no longer tenable. Our first understanding may prove to have been a misunderstanding.

For all that, what is to be gained from deliberative theological reflection cannot come by any other means. As Christians we are called to pursue growth in faith: by relearning and reinforcing what we already understand faith to be and by expanding, deepening, and even correcting our initial understandings of the faith. We are called to know God and ourselves more deeply and to pull together the consequences of that knowledge for our own lives and the world at large.

FOR FURTHER READING

Campbell, Ted A. *Christian Confessions: A Historical Introduction.* Louisville: Westminster John Knox Press, 1966. Campbell provides a lucid, one-volume comparison of the teachings of Christianity's major church traditions.

Jones, Linda, and Sophie Stanes. *In a Dark Wood: Journeys of Faith and Doubt.* Minneapolis: Fortress Press, 2003. This book tells of experiences in the region of doubt and recovery of faith among Jews, Catholics, and Protestants, women and men.

Kinast, Robert L. *What Are They Saying about Theological Reflection?* New York: Paulist Press, 2000. This is a brief but fine introduction to classical and contemporary discussions of theology. Kinast focuses especially on the experiential components of theological reflection.

McKim, Donald K., ed. *Westminster Dictionary of Theological Terms.* Louisville: Westminster John Knox Press, 1996. This is a reliable account of the familiar terms used by Christian theologians. It can be used to look up unfamiliar theological terms as well as to advance the reader toward better-informed, more deliberative theological thinking.

Musser, Donald W., and Joseph L. Price, eds. *New and Enlarged Handbook of Christian Theology.* Revised edition. Nashville: Abingdon Press, 2003. Presents informative articles on theology's standard and current topics, written by more than one hundred well-known contemporary theologians.

CHAPTER 2

FASHIONING THEOLOGY

FOR MUCH OF HISTORY, CRAFT HAS BEEN AN IMPOR-
tant function in human culture. The time-honored practice of
any craft (like that of garment makers, weavers, stone carvers, or
cabinetmakers) involves the fashioning of materials into an end
product through the exercise of skills that can be learned and per-
fected. They draw, measure, cut, assemble, glue, nail, stitch, pol-
ish, trim. To anyone unskilled in a craft, the results seem almost
magical; but its practitioners have developed their skill gradually
in some form of apprenticeship until they do it not only well, but
with apparent ease.

Theological reflection is in many respects comparable to a
craft. Like stone carvers or weavers, theologians work and rework
raw materials until they fashion a satisfactory end product—that
is, a theological understanding. The central operations they perform are three: (1) *interpreting* the meaning of Christian faith; (2)
correlating those interpretations with other interpretations; and
(3) *assessing* the adequacy of the interpretations and their correlations.

We will describe these three activities one by one, as tasks in
an orderly, cumulative process of reflection. Just as in any craft,
however, the operations interrelate and overlap. A woodworker
or seamstress measures before and after cutting and assembling,
tries and retries the assembly with each cut, resands, rebastes, or
trims to fit. Similarly, theologians, in interpreting, correlating, and
assessing, do not proceed in lockstep stages but constantly shift

back and forth among the operations, checking and adjusting in an effort to make the whole come together.

At the risk of pressing the analogy beyond its limits, we might observe that, while instructions can be given for the basic skills of the craft—woodworking, garment making, or theology—the distinction between a serviceable result and one that is truly superb all but defies prediction. It depends in part on the worker's hands and mind and in part on the eye of the beholder. Our embedded theology usually is serviceable . . . until, that is, our conscientiousness, or a crisis, or some conflict prompts second thoughts. It is then that the quest for something more satisfying sets us on the path of deliberative theology.

THEOLOGY AS INTERPRETING

At birth we enter a world of meaning-filled relations, and thereafter we make our way through that world by forming and re-forming interpretations of what things mean. All of us are ceaseless interpreters; that is, we are finders and givers of meanings. We interpret not only spoken and written words but also sights, sounds, textures, and smells, even tastes. The past and the future go into our interpretative mix as well—relics and memories of bygone times, anticipations of what tomorrow will bring. The interpretations we make become, in simplest terms, our *views.*

Our views arise so naturally in the course of interacting with others and the world around us that at first we take them for granted. As we mature, we discover that people interpret things differently. This realization dawns on us early—not because we have made a study of *hermeneutics* (the theory of interpretation) but because of the give-and-take of conversation, teaching and learning, disagreement and conflict.

Our awareness of differing interpretations of things is fed by encounters with others, and soon we notice our own interpretations changing over time. Views that seemed beyond question in childhood (or even last year) become less settled, and need to be reconfirmed or modified. We learn that there is more to the world of meaning than we have yet dreamed. Even if we harbor the secret conviction that there is a world of cold, hard facts for which one and only one true, universal, and abiding interpretation can be given, there is no denying that our life journey leads us through varied and often conflicting interpretations of things.

A number of views grouped into a more or less distinct set of interpretations comprise a *viewpoint,* or *perspective.* Our interpretations of what things mean are tied to our own particular angle of vision, just as other people interpret from angles of their own. But we are capable of shifting from one viewpoint to another. We may try to look at things from another's perspective or to examine

> Christian theological reflection interprets the meanings of things from the perspective of faith in the Christian message.

a matter from several differing standpoints—for instance, those of economics, ethics, politics, history, or others. As time goes by we grow more adept at moving among multiple interpretative viewpoints, comparing and contrasting and integrating them while taking stock of their relative merits.

Christian theological reflection interprets the meanings of things from the perspective of faith in the Christian message. Thus an interpretation of God and the nature of faith itself are of paramount concern to theology. Certain key themes of faith are universal topics of concern in the confessional statements and systematic theologies of all the church. For example, there is the doctrine of God, Christology (the doctrine of the person and work of Jesus Christ), pneumatology (the doctrine of the Holy Spirit), anthropology (the doctrine of human beings), soteriology (the doctrine of salvation), ecclesiology (the doctrine of the nature and purpose of the church), the doctrine of the authority and inspiration of Scripture, the doctrine of Christian life, and eschatology (the doctrine of last or final things).

The theological viewpoint that Christians form in the course of the life of faith is a distinctive set of many views, each relating in one way or another to the Christian message of God. Exactly what that message means is of primary concern to those seeking to understand their faith. In the church its substance is transmitted from generation to generation by means of the language of faith, a loose-knit collection of stories and symbols.

Learning how to use the language of faith is of critical importance in forming the set of interpretations that make up a theological perspective. Hence theologians routinely explore the range of meanings opened up to them by faith's language, using a wide variety of approaches and methods. Their theologies enunciate what they have come to understand the language of faith to mean.

THEOLOGY AS CORRELATING

Whatever approach theologians may take, the effort to expound the meaning of faith's language entails reckoning with multiple interpretative viewpoints. Theological thinking, therefore, involves *correlation*—that is, the process of bringing two or more discrete entities into mutual relation with each other. The correlation may occur between questions and their proposed answers, or among a variety of answers to a particular question.

The term *correlation* first came into popular use among theologians some decades ago with the writings of Paul Tillich, who urged that theology follow a "method of correlation." Tillich maintained that human life and culture raise questions of the ultimate

> Theological thinking involves correlation—the process of bringing two or more discrete entities into mutual relation with each other.

meaning of human existence to which religions and their theologies propose answers and that the task of theological reflection is to correlate these existential questions with their theological answers.

Tillich's account of the theological task generated considerable interest. It also sparked debate, for many feared that his method of correlation had the effect of trimming Christian theological convictions to fit comfortably with the wisdom of the world. The controversy has since passed into the history of theology, with only an occasional flare-up. This is not the place to speak for or against his method. Yet the term *correlation* remains a handy label for a complex process of comparison and contrast that takes place in all theological reflection, embedded and deliberative.

Even though theologians may quarrel with the notion of adhering to a formal method of correlation, the fact remains that theologians are inevitably correlators. They ascertain how a Christian view of things is similar to or compatible with views arising from other perspectives. At the same time, they identify the distinctiveness of a Christian viewpoint from all others by taking note of its differences from them.

Theologians cannot avoid correlating interpretations even if they swear never to do so. Correlating—in the generalized sense of the word—goes on even when it may pass without notice. For the most part, theological views are overlaid upon others that are nontheological. Who, for example, do we understand four-year-old Angelina to be? She is the natural daughter of Gilbert and Teresa, and the sister of Rita. This view of Angelina identifies her in terms of her place on her family tree. Yet of course she, like everyone and everything else, can be seen from other perspectives and described in other terms. She may be understood, when viewed by the eyes of faith and then described in theological terms, to be a child of God. In this case, the theological view of Angelina is a harmonious overlay upon the family-tree view; it accepts that Angelina is who the public views her to be, and then adds to this view the interpretation of her identity as a child of God. The overlay of interpretations acknowledges that Angelina means two different things at one time, just as overlapping red and blue lines on a map indicate a geographical feature, such as a river, that is also a political boundary between two states.

The example of who Angelina is may at first seem trivial, but real-life interpretative correlations are never to be taken lightly. Whose daughter Angelina is understood to be can be of great consequence, the decisive issue in an adoption or child custody suit. One couple, under indictment for the murder of their infant daughter, pleaded not guilty on the grounds that she was not their child but Satan's. Tragically, they had acted upon their interpretation of who the child was. Think, too, how often Christians have disputed—among themselves and with others—whose son they understand Jesus to be: God's? Mary's? Joseph's?

The correlation of interpretations is not always a harmonious, additive overlay of meanings. Differing points of view often lead to conflicting meanings. A ring, for example, may be worthless costume jewelry as viewed from the standpoint of a gemologist and yet mean true love to the one who wears it.

Consider the correlations made in a conflict that arose at First Church when the council took up the subject of the midwinter ski trip for young people. From a strictly budgetary perspective, it seemed good fiscal policy to require that those who wanted to go on the ski trip pay their own way. Some members, however, charged that the new rule meant favoritism and injustice, because it would exclude teens who came from families unable to come up with the money. After lengthy discussion, a compromise emerged. Since a church should be charitable as well as prudent with its funds, the budget could be stretched to cover expenses for those declaring themselves too needy to pay. But one critic of the policy then stumped the rest of them by asking, "What do ski trips have to do with the gospel anyway?" The associate pastor said a few words in favor of youth ministry, fellowship, good times, and Christian stewardship. But no explanation of exactly what aspect of the gospel's meaning commends church ski trips, pay-your-own-way or not, was forthcoming. In the end, the ski trip was scrapped altogether.

Were the critics simply opposed to the idea of young people having fun? Or had they glimpsed some theological aspect of the situation that everyone else had missed, or preferred to ignore?

Now and again Christians simply cannot bring themselves to see things as others do. There were Christians, for example, who would rather die than view the Roman emperor as divine. There are Christians who protest whenever people of any race or ethnic group are viewed as beasts or cannon fodder and not as human beings created in the image of God. And there are Christians, advocates of creationism and evolutionary theory alike, who, despite their differing views of Darwinism, join in common cause against the claim that human life has little value except as the survival of the fittest.

Our theological thinking has to do with interpreting the meaning of things. Theologians make their interpretations from the distinct perspective of faith in the Christian message; hence, similarities and differences between theological and other viewpoints on any given matter come to light by acts or correlation. In some cases the views may be mutually compatible and even supportive, but at other times so diametrically opposed that Christianity and culture find themselves locked in a bitter conflict of interpretations.

The correlation process takes place in many spheres and occurs at many levels. For example, what an environmentalist calls "caring for the ecosystem" may be correlated—that is, compared and contrasted—with the Christian view of good stewardship of God's creation. Theological views may be correlated to other views of social conditions, politics, medical ethics, education, parenting, economics, and so on. The Christian theological perspective as a

> The Christian theological perspective as a whole can be correlated to other overall life perspectives, such as those followed by adherents of the different world religions or proposed by various philosophers.

whole can be correlated to other overall life perspectives, such as those followed by adherents of the different world religions or proposed by various philosophers. For every Christian, correlating is at its base the task of relating theology to the circumstances of their lives, and vice versa.

Coming up with satisfactory correlations is by no means easy. The meanings joined to things from the culture press deeply upon church life. Even though the theological meaning of baptism, for example, has to do with God's grace and with commitment to the faith and the church, this interpretation may be eclipsed by social views that see the act as little other than a sentimental ceremony celebrating a baby's birth or a child's entry into adolescence. The morality taught by the church may simply reflect notions of good citizenship and the conventions of society rather than any well-considered theological judgment. Pastoral care and counseling is sometimes conducted from a strictly psychotherapeutic perspective without any reference to the resources of a theological viewpoint. In such instances the distinctive Christian identity of the church may be forgotten or lost entirely.

Appeals for a return to tradition or recovery of the language of faith are often offered as correctives to the cultural captivity of the churches. So long as it does not serve merely to substitute one form of cultural captivity for another, the effort to mine the church's theological heritage for whatever guidance it has to offer people today is wholesome.

Much of the language of faith may seem—even to many Christians—a foreign tongue; rather than aiding them in interpreting the meaning of things, it is itself a riddle. Lacking terms for describing the distinctiveness of their faith perspective, modern Christians are prone to stammer, improvise, or go with the flow of what passes for wisdom.

Using traditional language is not itself a guarantee that the meaning of faith is rightly understood. The vitality of theology cannot be assured just by repeating well-worn religious phrases. The meaning of the historic language of the faith needs to be unlocked by acts of interpretation and correlation that disclose the significance of things in relationship to the message of God. Otherwise Christians may end up sounding like a noisy gong or clanging cymbal.

Indeed, theologians are often blindsided by complaints that their faith interpretations are empty, with no apparent correlation to the daily living of the faith. Alienated Christians are often heard to say: "The trouble with the church is, all I hear there are pious phrases without any connection to the real world I live in."

Laypersons may grumble: "The trouble with ministers is, they're out of touch with the real world. Their ivory-tower theologies don't speak to the problems I have to face as a Christian."

Pastors now and again complain: "The trouble with seminary professors is, they don't know what's going on in the church. Their ivory-tower theologies don't speak to the problems I have to deal with as a Christian minister."

Professors in the practical fields sometimes echo the complaint: "My colleagues in the classical fields don't seem to know what church and ministry are all about. Their ivory-tower lectures don't relate to the real problems that ministers must face."

Professors in the classical fields have been heard to respond: "It's beyond me how anyone can expect to do ministry without dealing with what I'm trying to teach and write about [in biblical studies, history, theology, or ethics]. My job is to help students come to grips with the most serious and profound issues of religious faith ever."

The quest for relevance can become an obsession leading to trendiness or burnout. Yet the whole point of theology is to *understand the meaning of God's message to the world today.* The point of correlating theological and nontheological views is to identify what things mean in relation to that message so that Christians may carry out their life of service keenly aware of its distinctiveness.

THEOLOGY AS ASSESSMENT

A theological perspective is only one of many differing viewpoints in a society, yet it is of paramount value to the one who holds it. Its value is rooted in the conviction that what is disclosed through the eyes of Christian faith is of great importance.

Some embedded theologies may at times signal this confident assessment of reality in shorthand, even abrupt fashion. "Believe or be damned," "Faith can't be proved," "The Bible/pope/creed/church says . . ." are commonplace responses when a particular theological view is questioned. (Of course, many Christians express the strength of their convictions more gently and modestly.) Offering some evaluation of the *rationale* and *trustworthiness* of a theology is an integral part of the reflective theological enterprise.

When our initial understandings seem no longer tenable, when we must decide among several conflicting understandings of faith, deliberative theologies develop as the result of self-consciously weighing alternative theological views. If we proceed

> When our initial understandings seem no longer tenable, when we must decide among several conflicting understandings of faith, deliberative theologies develop as the result of self-consciously weighing alternative theological views.

reflectively, we will give careful thought to the standards of judgment, that is, the theological criteria, used in assessing the views we take. Given, for example, that some understand Christian faith to permit capital punishment and others do not, what is our view of the matter? A conscientious decision will involve weighing various pro-and-con arguments. It will also require that we identify the criteria we use to decide between these contradictory understandings. To engage in theological reflection on such an issue is to seek clarity not only about the relative merits of each option but even about how we determine what counts as a merit.

Several types of assessment are used in theological reflection. Inasmuch as theology has to do with faith seeking understanding, the theologian aims to attain the most complete and accurate understanding possible. It is the very adequacy of a theology that is assessed. Several considerations are taken into account in making such an assessment. Four of the most common tests of adequacy deserve brief comment: Christian appropriateness, intelligibility, moral integrity, and validity.

(1) *Christian appropriateness* evaluates a theology in light of its "Christianness," that is, its faithfulness to the Christian message. What is it about faith in the Christian message of God that commends this theological view rather than some other? This was the test that sank the ski trip at First Church: when push came to shove, no one demonstrated that there was anything "Christian" about it. In like manner, every theological view is subject to an assessment regarding whether or not it is something worthy of Christian commitment.

(2) *Intelligibility* is the concern that a Christian theology makes sense to Christians even if to no one else. One way of showing intelligibility is logical consistency. Some have sought such consistency by developing a theology that begins with one single concept (for instance, the idea of God or the idea of revelation) and then carefully unfolds its logical implications. But few theologies are strictly logical—not least because the language of faith is so diverse and paradoxical that it defies logical forms. The more realizable goal is *plausible coherence*—a degree of cohesiveness in the multifaceted meaning of Christian faith and the avoidance of contradictory messages.

(3) *Moral integrity* is concerned with a theology's ethical standards. Christian faith is, in addition to believing and heartfelt feeling, a way of living guided by moral values. The field of Christian ethics makes the moral dimension of the Christian message of God its primary focus. All theological writings, regardless of the topic on which they focus, contain indications of the theologian's ethical sensitivity. Thus an assessment of theological views in terms of their moral integrity plays a role in coming to a judgment about their overall adequacy.

Assessments of this sort sometimes seem easy to make. Today at least, Christians recoil in horror to hear of some theologian who calls the church to persecute or exterminate unbelievers. Such a view, virtually everyone agrees, is repugnant to all for which the faith stands. This theologian's god is too ruthless to be the God of Christian faith.

At other times, moral assessments may prompt much soul-searching and controversy. Moral questions often surface in debates over the doctrine of predestination, for example. Critics have asked

> In their assessment, theologies that fail to address the world's manifold forms of suffering also fail to honor God's moral integrity.

how the God of love could ever be said to doom some and save others before their birth. Defenders of the doctrine have sought to show not only its Christian aptness but how it upholds the sovereignty of God's decisions about justice and mercy.

The moral integrity of God is also important to most present-day liberation theologians. Without denying the universality of God's love, they note that the God of the Scriptures repeatedly opposes bigotry, injustice, and oppression and stands for the downtrodden of the world. In their assessment, theologies that fail to address the world's manifold forms of suffering also fail to honor God's moral integrity.

(4) *Validity.* The question of validity has to do with the credibility, reality, and truth of theological views. When Christians set forth their theology (their understanding of what faith means), they do so out of a conviction that their affirmations of belief are true to life and God's intentions and will. Surely there are those who consider some or all of our theological views to be unfounded and illusory. Just as surely, most of us consider our own views to be true and those of others who differ from us to be false. Assessing the validity of theology, whether our own or that of others, is inevitable. We do it all the time.

Explaining why a theological view is valid is perhaps the most difficult task that theologians face. Whether a theology even should be tested for its validity is itself much disputed. On the one side is a mixed company of theologians who agree among themselves on little more than that theology's work is done once it has set forth the meaning of faith in the Christian message of God as accurately and fully as possible. This suffices, they argue, because efforts to assess the validity of theology invariably end up judging God's message by human standards of credibility, reality, and truth. On the other side is an equally diverse group of theologians who insist that Christians should not sidestep testing the claims of faith. Even though the results cannot prove faith itself, they indicate where adjustments are called for—either in our human theological understanding of faith or in our human standards of credibility, reality, and truth.

Assessing the adequacy of a theology—in terms of its Christian appropriateness, intelligibility, moral integrity, and validity—is a complex and crucial matter. When professional theologians write to one another about it, what they say is frequently difficult for nonspecialist readers to grasp. This is not because the theologians' faith is deeper or their understanding of the issue higher than anyone else's. Nor is it because they do not care about various specific, practical issues that laypeople and ministers face every day. They are concerned about how to judge the adequacy of a theological belief. Rather than directly arguing for or against capital punishment or predestination, they may focus on the criteria used to decide the issue. And in so doing they resort to a terminology that is usually too abstract and technical for use in worship, church school, or everyday conversation about the meaning of faith.

Assessment itself, however, is not at all remote from theological discussion in the church and public life. It is simply carried out in very down-to-earth terms. "Is it Christian?" is a common concern of church members who question the *appropriateness* of a particular view. The matter of *intelligibility* arises whenever someone's theological statements leave listeners or readers bewildered by what has just been said. *Moral integrity* often surfaces in gut-level responses to some Christian's theological views. (The Anderson family, for example, left the church after the preacher commented that God would show no mercy to a teenager who had a baby out of wedlock. "That preacher's God," they said, "is too hateful to be God at all.") Issues of *validity* arise whenever theological views come into conflict with what has come to be accepted generally as truth. (Do archaeology and historical research back up the biblical story of Noah's flood or the empty tomb of the crucified Jesus? If Freud is right about the ego, superego, and the id, where is what Christians call the soul to be found? When an evangelist plays on the emotions of the audience, claiming that God will rain financial blessing on all who accept Jesus today, is that pitch valid because it works—that is, it has the effect of leading scores to come forward to become Christian?)

Christians are not reticent about expressing their opinions on such matters, and on countless others. In doing so they are assessing the adequacy of the correlated interpretations of Christian faith that they encounter. But if assessments are to be made on more than an ad hoc, ill-informed, and inconsistent basis, all Christian theologians need to give thought to the standards of judgment that they apply. They need to fashion their theology as carefully as the stonemason crafted a medieval cathedral, or a woodworker crafts a fine cabinet, or a weaver crafts a fine piece of cloth. Their embedded theology and their readings and conversations with others are the raw material they work with; native intelligence and sensitivity are their talent. But it takes skill, practiced and honed over time, to make a useful and adequate theology.

FOR FURTHER READING

Jones, Serene, and Paul Lakeland, eds. *Constructive Theology: A Contemporary Approach to Classical Themes*. Minneapolis: Fortress Press, 2004. From the Workgroup of Constructive Christianity Theology come contributions by a diverse array of theologians that consider the church's theological heritage and the challenges of formulating Christian teachings in today's world. Includes CD-ROM.

Kelsey, David H. *Proving Doctrine: The Uses of Scripture in Modern Theology*. Harrisburg, Pa.: Trinity Press International, 1999. One of Christianity's most distinguished scholars, Kelsey casts light on the ways modern theologians view the authority of the Bible as they formulate their theological views.

McKim, Donald K. *Theological Turning Points: Major Issues in Christian Thought*. Atlanta: Westminster John Knox Press, 1988. McKim highlights several influential doctrinal disputes in the history of the church and describes how theologically opposing sides drew upon Scripture, tradition, reasoning, and experience to defend what they held to be important.

Ruggiero, Vincent. *The Art of Thinking: A Guide to Critical and Creative Thought.* Seventh edition. New York: Pearson/Longman, 2004. Theological thinking is thinking as well as theology. Ruggiero's work is a popular and newly updated introduction to thinking and writing in a critical and creative fashion.

CHAPTER 3

RESOURCES FOR THEOLOGICAL REFLECTION

YEARS AGO ONE OF US OWNED AN ANCIENT, AILING Renault Dauphine. It was always falling apart, but was the most this college student could afford. The car was nicknamed "Luther" because of his famous statement, "Here I stand." And this is what "Luther" frequently did—until, one subzero January night, it made its last trip at the end of a towrope behind a relative's Buick.

Martin Luther's refusal to recant his theology may seem brave to some, obstinate to others. In any case, it alerts us to an important point about theology. He could not back down because, among other things, he could not stand anywhere else than where his life-long journey of faith had led him.

So it is with all theologians. Like every undertaking, theological reflection begins by necessity *where we stand.* In effect we are saying, "This to the best of my understanding is what Christian faith means." It is our individual and collective experience of God at work in our lives, in the church, and in the world that causes us to reflect on that experience theologically. We set out from where we are, continuing along the path of faith consciously seeking greater understanding.

As Christians we should know that we are not alone on this venture. There are others like us—some who have gone before, some ready to follow in their own good time, and some waiting only for us to give them a nod. We should know that we are not left to our own devices. Help is available. Provisions, perhaps more ample than we suspect, exist in our embedded theology. More are available by drawing upon the sources from which that theology emerged. Still others are to be found along the way.

FROM THEOLOGICAL VIEWPOINT TO THEOLOGICAL TEMPLATE

Christians already have a theological viewpoint, an angle of vision on the world that is part and parcel of their faith in the Christian message. To view things theologically is to identify, correlate, and assess their meaning in light of their relationship to that message. In moving from embedded to deliberative theology, we become aware—perhaps for the first time—that our theological viewpoint functions as a *template,* not unlike those used in fields other than theology.

Templates of the Mind

The human mind operates with certain indispensable structures or schemata that organize and make sense of data received by the senses. Psychologists using a Rorschach test, for example, know that the brain organizes the inkblot design in light of one's experiences, emotions, and intellect; for one person the image brings to mind a beautiful mountain scene, while for another the same inkblot may suggest genitalia. These structures of the mind, which we will call *templates,* are essential for organizing information into a manageable whole.

To illustrate: Through years of education, training, and practical experience, a physician acquires a *medical template.* Without it a correct diagnosis of health or illness would be impossible. A patient comes into the office and says, "I've been feeling light-headed lately, mostly when I'm standing up." The physician consults her chart and finds that the patient is taking medications for high blood pressure, and so asks a few simple questions about body positions and movements, fatigue, stress, and hearing. While talking with the patient in plain unsophisticated language, however, the physician is filtering every response through a refined medical template. It is second nature; there is hardly any need for conscious recall. "Short of breath—aha, periodic hyperventilation . . . indica-tions and contraindications relative to alternative anti-hypertensive drugs . . . revised dosage levels to be considered, orthostatic hyper-tension . . ." and so forth. This medical template—a grid of analyti-cal terms and diagnostic categories—is overlaid upon the patient's simple words and the doctor's clinical observations. It organizes them into a medically meaningful whole that includes diagnosis of the likely problem and its treatment. Back home again, the patient tells the family: "I'm fine; I just have to take some red pills instead of those terrible green ones."

The template of medical doctors, like those of skilled workers in other fields of endeavor, is forged from the accumulated learn-ing and reflection that is unique to their particular discipline. No template can be regarded as final and definitive in the sense that it captures the meaning of things in their entirety.

Nor does anyone rely on the use of one template alone. Respon-sible physicians, for example, will apply other templates (psycholog-ical, sociological, legal, religious) along with the strictly medical one before making up their minds about the patient's condition. Yet it would be irresponsible—grounds for a malpractice suit—to reject or ignore the template that they are specifically trained to use.

Theological Templates

Christians who engage in theological reflection operate with a theological template that sorts and organizes the data of life. They use their template to identify how things are, make a prognosis of what is likely to happen, and settle on a prescription (a theo-logical proposal) regarding that for which faith calls. It is the lens through which they look at the world. Each Christian as theolo-gian has one. Each template is distinct from the templates of other Christian theologians, as well as those of other religious, political,

Christians who engage in theological reflection operate with a theologi-cal template that sorts and organizes the data of life.

or cultural movements; it is a pattern of theological meanings that interprets, correlates, and assesses things in relationship to faith in the Christian message of God.

Perhaps the easiest way to recognize the key to a theologian's template or to discover your own embedded theological template is to look for what is emphasized. Every theologian operates with a certain set of core theological views—favored images, categories, and themes. These primary theological views stand in the foreground, against a backdrop of the theologian's other, less central notions. Or, changing our metaphor to music, we might liken the key ingredients in the makeup of a theological template to melody lines: less crucial elements are the notes of harmony or counterpoint.

The term *faith*, for example, is part of the theological template repeatedly used in this book's discussion of theological reflection. Most readers have caught on to that by now, considering how often the term appears. But the elements of a template are not only a matter of frequency. (Even though angels are mentioned fifty times in a Christmas Eve sermon, they may be of little importance in the preacher's theological template.)

Elements of a template are identifiable by their *functions*: they are the points by which theologians take their bearings in order to set a course of interpretation, correlation, and assessment. Thus we have spoken of faith as a multifaceted reality that is at once personal and communal; that embraces belief, action, and feeling; that seeks understanding; and so on. What makes the word *faith* part of the template used in this book is not the frequency of its use, but its function. On one hand, it brings together seemingly unrelated images and concepts. On the other hand, it distinguishes things that might at first appear to be inseparably linked. Other theologians, using templates other than ours, might not put "faith" to such heavy use. They may prefer another theme, perhaps a close synonym like "the Christian life"—or a pattern of thematic emphases wholly different from ours.

All Christians operate with a theological template. Responsible theologians, like responsible physicians, seek to be of service to others and make use of their template believing it to be beneficial. They are also mindful of how many factors it takes into account, and of its limits. The template may well be the best one available. But there is always more to be learned not only from professional schooling and continuing education but also from daily practice.

Input from a variety of sources contributes to the development of a seasoned theologian.

In recent years, it seems, the theologian's template has become even more eclectic than that of the physician. Theological reflection has lost much of its credibility in the intellectual community. Many pastors are tempted to discard the theological template altogether in favor of a secular template—political, sociological, or psychological—that they think is more contemporary. What is regrettable is not Christians' use of other templates (no more than a doctor's use of a variety of templates in considering a patient's treatment), but their ignoring of the theological template. In effect they are selling their birthright.

All Christians need to operate with a theological template. Without it, spiritual assessment of what is happening with a trou-

> A Christian theological template affords resources, insight, and an angle of vision that no other template can provide.

bled parishioner, or in one's Christian life, will surely result in an inadequate theological response. A Christian theological template affords resources, insight, and an angle of vision that no other template can provide. Lacking a theological template, contemporary Christian theologians (all of us) are liable to repeat the information and alleged "wisdom" of the dominant culture and ignore the singular Christian message of God.

A theological template, like any other, is not a rigid conceptual framework. It is simply a way of organizing our reflections about what happens to us and those for whom we care. Correlating one's theology with one's personal ministry in concrete situations—with our students, coworkers, children, parishioners, and friends, even strangers who need our care—is a dynamic process of making our theology concrete in every moment of our life.

RESOURCES

What elements go into developing a theological template? The most important, to judge by a study of embedded and deliberative theologies, are four: Scripture, tradition, reason, and experience. In recent years many have come to know this foursome as "the Methodist quadrilateral." Members of that denomination will surely permit us to borrow and adapt the phrase for more general use here. It serves to clarify concerns widely shared by the worldwide community of faith.

It may seem unusual, we admit, to label Scripture, tradition, reason, and experience as the *resources* Christians incorporate into their theological template. Typically they are called theology's *sources* or *authorities.* Whether theologians should rely on all four or only one or two of them is a matter of long-standing controversy, and calling them resources rather than sources or authorities does not settle the issue. Nor is it meant to. Our aim in reviewing these four resources is to aid the efforts of Christians who seek to become theologically deliberative.

The history of theology shows that theologians are rarely if ever untouched by the influence of all four resources, whether or not they acknowledge their influence. How could it be otherwise? Theological reflection can never be isolated from the life setting of faith. Whatever that setting may be, elements of Scripture, tradition, reason, and experience have already found some place in it. These elements go into the makeup of the template that theologians use in deciding the questions of faith.

It seems to follow that, in studying someone else's theology as well as forming our own, it is important to observe where these resources are used and the relative weight given to each. Theological reflection is far too complex and subtle for simplistic summaries. Determining how these resources figure in one's theology requires careful and thorough consideration.

Scripture

Scholars have sometimes described Christianity as a "religion of the book." Some years ago, German theologian Gerhard Ebeling wrote that "church history is the history of the exposition of Scripture."[1] He reminded us that the collection of writings which Christians call the Holy Bible is an integral element in the life of the church, and in Christian theology as well. Theologians sometimes accuse one another of underestimating or overestimating the value of Scripture, mistaking its meaning, or failing to apply it rightly. These disputes, however, are usually domestic quarrels; no serious theologian denies that Scripture is vitally important in the household of faith.

Christianity is a history-based religion; one of the chief values of Scripture is that it speaks of that history. Virtually all that is known of the origins of Christianity is recorded in the books of the New Testament. Other references to this faith, including writings not included in the New Testament, furnish additional glimpses into Christianity's origins; welcome as these are, they are of limited use except by comparison with the biblical texts.

The Christian biblical canon familiar to us today (with Hebrew Scripture and New Testament writings) is a legacy of the ancient church. It emerged from a consensus formed over several centuries and reflects the impact these books had on church life. In a strictly historical sense, then, the Bible and the church belong together, and theologians whose faith seeks understanding must return to the witness of the Scriptures.

> The Scriptures proclaim the Word that called forth the faith of Israel and the faith of the earliest Christians.

The significance of the Bible for theology, however, cannot be reduced to its value as a historical record. Christians seek to hear through these writings a message from God—the Word of God. The Scriptures proclaim the Word that called forth the faith of Israel and the faith of the earliest Christians. That Word of God is still heard today by the reading of Scripture. It is not surprising that these writings have a special status in the church and exert a special force—a canonical force—on theological thinking. They contain resources essential for theologians whose aim is to understand the meaning of the faith. For many Protestants especially, a phrase from the Reformation expresses their abiding conviction: the Bible is *norma normans sed non normata,* the norm that judges every other norm but is not itself judged by any other.

Other Christians maintain that the phrase *norma normans sed non normata* goes too far. They point to the human and historically limited character of the biblical writings. They note that many influences come into play, unconsciously as well as consciously, as theologians go about constructing their theologies and evaluating those of others. They suggest that it is virtually impossible for any theologian to certify that he or she will work with only *x* number of norms, one of which will be judged by none other. They add that it is dangerous not to subject any of theology's resources to cross-examination lest the system of checks and balances in theological reflection be set out of kilter. For reasons such as these, there are those who speak of the status and usefulness of the Bible for theology in terms other than *norma normans.*

The use of Holy Scripture in theology has always been a hot-button issue in theology: its authority, inspiration, unity and diversity, and reliability in terms of history and faith have been particular areas of concern. Each church has its own viewpoint on these matters, and there is considerable grassroots diversity as well. Each of us is well advised to consider where we will stand on these questions. However, we should not stop at stating our beliefs about the Bible. How we make use of the Bible's resources in actual practice is another important question. Theologian David Kelsey, in *Proving Doctrine: The Uses of Scripture in Recent Theology,* points to four distinct ways in which modern theologians draw biblical texts into their theological reflections.[2] (He states that these four ways are not meant to be exhaustive.) While the authority of Scripture is affirmed in all four cases, the Word of God heard through the words of the Bible is identified in different ways: as (1) propositions about divine truth, (2) symbolic expressions of faith experiences, (3) recitals of God's identity, or (4) invitations to existential possibilities for new life.

Try listening for Kelsey's categories in the next sermon you hear. When the minister quotes Scripture, ask yourself: What is this speaker using the Bible to ask me to do? Or, put the same question to a sermon or lesson that you deliver: What are you asking your hearers to do when you quote the Bible?

Veterans as well as newcomers to theology will be relieved to hear that no theologian can be expected to sort out everything involved in making use of Scripture before daring to make a theological statement. Clearly, however, theologians who are at all deliberative recognize that the choices they face in trying to evaluate or construct a theology do not amount simply to quoting Bible verses. Appraisals of the use of Scripture and its proper interpretation are matters of considerable complexity.

Although it may be impossible to resolve all of the complexities before constructing a theological viewpoint, two concerns deserve careful thought. The first has to do with the *responsible interpretation* of Scripture. The biblical text does not speak for itself; every reading is someone's interpretation of it. The actual analysis of its meaning is called *exegesis*. (Readings that impose our own ideas on Scripture instead of the meaning that is there are *eisegesis*.) The principles of interpretation that guide exegesis are referred to as *biblical hermeneutics*. Exegetical practices and hermeneutical approaches have varied widely from age to age. All theologians should be intentional about the way they read the biblical texts.

The second, related concern has to do with the way we handle the diversity of views *within* the Scriptures. Although it comes bound between two covers, the Bible is not one book, strictly speaking, but an anthology of books written over many centuries, each reflecting its own distinctive origins addressing its own distinctive context. What is more, amid the variety of books is a diversity in the use of language—images, metaphors, poetry, historical narrative, cultic materials, legal and oral prescriptions, prophetic, sermonic, and didactic passages.

This diversity enhances the value of the Bible to the church, for it provides a rich storehouse of materials proclaiming the faith from many different angles. It also poses a major challenge. Those who read the Bible in order to hear God's message to the world have to make decisions about how its diverse contents contribute to that message. Often an appeal to what one passage says on a particular subject can be met by a counterclaim based on another passage that says something different. The tendency for people to pick and choose portions of the Bible to support their own favored views—often called proof-texting—is so familiar that, as the saying goes, "you can prove anything from the Bible."

Is there an alternative to proof-texting? Drawing on the resources of Scripture in the course of theological reflection calls for deciding how the parts relate to the whole and vice versa. It helps to learn as much as possible about the Bible as a whole while remaining attentive to the individuality of each book.

It also helps to look for prominent themes—creation, covenant, law, judgment, promise, prophecy, Jesus, sin, salvation, gospel, the church, to name a few. Consider how the themes are developed and what you perceive to be points of connection among them. Throughout church history, theologians have sought to develop an overall scheme for ordering Scripture's diversity of voices. Be on the lookout for the scheme (if any) of the theologians you hear or read about: what they emphasize, what they ignore, and how they weave threads from Scripture into an overall pattern. By evaluating their efforts in light of your own ongoing study of the Bible, you can construct a responsible approach to the use of Scripture for theological deliberation.

Tradition

One way to guard against getting caught up in the implicit theologies of the present culture, or being blown along by the latest wind of doctrine, is to take seriously the resources of tradition. Tradition has to do both with the process of passing something from one age to another and with the something that is passed on. Churches always have sought to preserve the basic truths of faith intact as they are transmitted from person to person and generation to generation. The message of God's good news is to be shared with all, to the end of time. Passing along this message is the dynamic process of active tradition.

Tradition is also thought of as the sum total of what the church has passed down over time. Not only the content of the Christian message of God but also the teachings, writings, rituals, and customs of the church are referred to as tradition. The term has become a virtual synonym for the church's past.

The meaning of tradition was at the forefront of the great Reformation debates over the interrelationship of Scripture and tradi-

> The Spirit guides the church throughout history to maintain the truths of faith by developing other traditions that help convey the Christian message.

tion. Early Protestants, emphasizing the importance of Scripture, insisted on testing every church tradition against the standards of the biblical writings. A distinction was drawn: whereas Scripture is of divine origin, traditions are human and fallible and hence reformable.

The Roman Catholic affirmation was "Scripture *and* tradition," intending not to discount Scripture but to deny a strict separation of the two. Tradition had a more important place in its theology. It was believed that the same Spirit who inspired the writing of the Scriptures also inspired the apostles to pass on oral instructions about the church. The Spirit guides the church throughout history to maintain the truths of faith by developing other traditions that help convey the Christian message. And the same Spirit, alive in the community of faith, enables Christians to understand the authority and meaning of the Bible rightly within the context of the church's tradition.

History often takes surprising turns. Renewed concern for the Scriptures is a striking feature of Roman Catholic theology in the twentieth century, especially since the Second Vatican Council. At the same time, Protestant scholars have come to a greater appreciation of tradition, recognizing that biblical texts are largely recordings of the oral traditions of Israel and the early church. If there ever was a time when the difference between Protestant and Catholic could be boiled down simply to Scripture versus tradition, that time has long since passed.

Though often unacknowledged in practice, tradition has played almost as prominent a role in Protestantism as in Roman Catholicism. Protestants become Protestants—and Catholics become Catholics—because of what has been passed on to them by their churches. Each Christian denomination honors its heritage, encourages its members to remain loyal to it, and commends it to initiates.

Many denominations hold historic creeds, confessions of faith, and catechisms to be of special significance for theological reflection. In such cases faithfulness to the tradition of church teaching is understood to go hand in hand with faithfulness to the witness of Scripture. Others disavow any official, churchwide theological standards, confident that their tradition of reliance on the Scriptures leads to teachings which preserve the essentials of authentic faith while maximizing freedom on other inessential points.

The theological resources of tradition are not confined to formal statements about church doctrine. There are traditions of practice that are an important resource for theological reflection in certain churches. Traditions of worship, prayer, poetry, hymnody, visual arts, and religious drama are examples. Sometimes a simple action, or the refrain of a hymn, can yield greater insight into the meaning of faith than could any thick theological tome.

Christians, as theologians, cannot accept *everything* tradition has to offer. Some elements of tradition do not deserve to be called resources for theological reflection. They are trivialities, liabilities, nasty habits—or even poisons, harmful to Christians and other living things. Deliberative theologians should give heed to the warning: "Sift tradition with care before use."

The dynamic process of passing on the Christian message involves an interplay of continuity and change. Whatever is handed over from one context to another is subject to reinterpretation. The difficulty arises when new forms are required to communicate theological constructs that were once expressed by other means. And, as times change, words or actions that remain the same may take on new meaning while shedding facets of their original significance. Clearly, tradition is dynamic. It is a living, growing resource for theological reflection that provides a glimpse of the ongoing work of God in the world.

Reason

At various times in history, theologians have relied upon reason to supply certain truths accessible to all people as rational beings. Claims about the truths of reason in this comprehensive sense are rare today. (The prevailing tendency is to think of reason as a tool for dealing with theological resources.) The usefulness of reason as a theological resource has to do with taking care in how we think about things.

The standards for what constitutes sound reasoning are disputed. The precision of formal logic and mathematics is sometimes held up as the ideal, and some theologians have made attempts to model theology along the lines of the "hard" or social sciences, following the scientific method of reasoning and seeking equally assured results. Other theologians, however, point out that matters of faith are not rightly understood in scientific terms. They suggest that the scientific method is not as certain as it is often reputed to be. They urge theologians to reason well using means other than those of scientists.

In any case, reasoning is part of theological reflection. It is involved in interpreting Scripture, tradition, and experience. It also plays a role in every effort to assess alternative accounts of the Christian faith in search of the most adequate one. And reason is essential in attempting to explain why one theological view is preferable to others. Although unanimity with respect to the nature and criteria of good reasoning will never be achieved, theologians who ignore this one rule of thumb are at risk: *theology needs to be as clear, coherent, and well informed as possible.*

The term *well informed* reminds us that in a broad sense reason is a source of information. The wide variety of inquiries carried out in the natural sciences, social sciences, history, philosophy, and even literature and the arts provides us with a vast array of information about the world. Theologians cannot avoid addressing this store of information. Although all may not accept the informa-

> Theologians who ignore this one rule of thumb are at risk: *theology needs to be as clear, coherent, and well informed as possible.*

tion, it is too much a part of the fabric of our lives to be ignored. Views based on reason in this sense must be taken into account in attempting to set forth the meaning of the Christian message for our present day. Only by this means is it possible to identify that message's meaning today, much less to speak of its distinctiveness.

Experience

Experience plays a significant role in theological reflection. Sometimes it is granted a leading role, equal to or beyond that of other resources; explicit references to experience justifying theological claims are prominent in such theologies. In other cases, experience's role is likely to work behind the scenes. Whatever the case, experience deserves consideration as a resource for theological reflection.

All of life—and the life of faith—is a matter of experiencing. Every moment is a moment of experience with bodily, sensory, intellectual, emotional, and spiritual aspects: waking up, going to sleep, reading a good novel or the Bible, voting, dreaming, resisting bigotry, cleaning up the house, even breathing. The life of faith embraces the totality of our life experiences. And although the Scriptures hardly ever call them experiences, this is the umbrella term used by theologians for the varied encounters with God, and for the awareness of God that comes through faith to the people of

> An experience is always an experience *of something*. It is this something, disclosed through our experiences, that is taken up into our theological reflections.

Israel, to New Testament Christians, and to us today. In this sense, experiences of God are indispensable resources for theology.

Yet the term *experience* can be misleading. The report that "I just had an experience" is not in itself a resource for theology. An experience is always an experience *of something*. It is this something, disclosed through our experiences, that is taken up into our theological reflections. Through our experience of reading or hearing the Scriptures, for example, God's Word of mercy may be disclosed to us. Through prayer experiences, the comforting and uplifting presence of the Spirit may come to be known more fully. Through the experience of struggling for social justice, the contrast between the holiness of God and oppressive powers of this world is exposed. Firsthand experiences such as these contribute to our understanding of the faith. And what we have learned firsthand enhances our theology and helps contribute to the theological reflection of others as well.

The experiences of individuals as well as communities figure in discussions of the Christian life. Remarkable spiritual experiences by people of faith have had an impact on the history of theology. Some theologians, for example, have used the story of Paul's conversion on the Damascus road as a paradigm for the Christian conversion experience. Experiences associated with the devotion to Mary, including accounts of apparitions of Mary, have fostered the Roman Catholic Church's teaching on Mariology (the doctrine of Mary). A vision of a reunited church led Episcopal Bishop Charles H. Brent to pioneer the twentieth-century ecumenical movement.

The church has always been on guard against accepting every alleged experience of God as genuine. Some claims to direct, special experiences of God deserve attention because they teach theologians to guard against self-styled messengers of God with revelations other than the gospel. Church history is filled with such claims: the tragic results of such claims at Jonestown and at Waco are infamous examples. Individual religious experiences need not be remarkable in order to be theologically significant, but all experience needs rigorous theological testing.

The corporate experiences of the community of faith also play a role in theological reflection. In some cases, these experiences go hand in hand with specific theological traditions—for example, emphasis on gifts of the Spirit in Holiness and Pentecostal traditions; social concern for justice among the historic African American churches; participation in the mysteries of God through liturgical worship in Roman Catholic and Orthodox communions. In other cases, community experiences cut across denominational boundaries. For instance, Christians in those communities that have experienced persecution or poverty or exclusion—whether in society or in the church itself—may well find themselves in a position to witness to aspects of the Christian faith that people in more comfortable circumstances have been unable or unwilling to discern. The theological witnesses of women and minorities come most readily to mind. Their reflections, emerging from experiences of marginalization, injustice, and unquenchable hope, command attention from those whose views have so long dominated theological discussions.

Experience often serves as a reality check against overblown and false theological assertions. A certain televangelist, for example, made a fortune for himself by telling his audience that if they would surrender their hearts and bank accounts to God (the funds to be sent in care of the televangelist's post office box), they would assuredly prosper. Testimonials came from folks who gained riches after giving large sums of money to his ministry. But the experience of many generous donors who stayed in poverty—or became impoverished because of their donations—gave the lie to this bogus theology.

The reality check that experience offers to theology cannot be appreciated only by citing examples of bunco artists masquerading as theologians. All theologians—the writers and readers of the Scriptures, the makers of tradition and those who later seek to uphold it—must be cognizant that they occupy a specific place in a specific context. They experience themselves, the world, and the message of God within this context. Their theologies may—with their socially located experience—witness to genuine, lasting elements of faith's meaning.

Attention to faith experiences of other Christians in different social locations is one means to test the truth of theological understandings that we come to hold. Hard-nosed social analysis of the experience-based assumptions operating upon any given theologian, along the lines of the social sciences, is another way to test the validity of our theological reflection.

Theological reflection makes use of resources derived from experience. Theology has experiential roots. Doing theological reflection calls for Christians to be aware of the experience factor in their own understandings of the faith, and the understandings of faith of others.

Resources for theological reflection are many and varied. Those who engage in theological reflection will want to inspect the mix of resources a theologian brings to bear on any given issue. How well does the template capture and disclose the meaning of Christian faith? What is missed or distorted by its use? They will also want, in developing their own theological position, to give thought to the recipe they follow in mixing these ingredients for themselves.

In short, Christian theologians are called upon to attend to the makeup of their theological template. Does it draw upon the resources of Scripture, tradition, reason, and experience? Are those resources used responsibly? We need a template that will bring those resources to bear upon our interpretation, correlation, and assessment of the meaning of things from the viewpoint of faith in the Christian message of God.

FOR FURTHER READING

Allen, Diogenes. *Philosophy for Understanding Theology*. Louisville: Westminster John Knox Press, 1985. Perhaps no one in recent decades has been more helpful in introducing philosophy-free theologians to what they need to know about "philosophy and theology" than Allen.

Anderson, William P., ed. *A Journey through Christian Theology, with Texts from the First to the Twenty-First Century*. Minneapolis: Fortress Press, 2000. This book provides the reader with an opportunity to follow the historic course of Christian theological conversation.

Collins, John J. *Introduction to the Hebrew Bible*. Minneapolis: Fortress Press, 2004; and Theissen, Gerd. *Fortress Introduction to the New Testament*. Minneapolis: Fortress Press, 2003. No one has to wait around for scholars to expound on the meaning of the Bible, but Christians seeking growth in understanding will welcome the insights of sound critical books on the subject. Many are available; various churches have their denominational preferences. These are two well-known, ecumenically oriented volumes.

Fitchett, George. *Assessing Spiritual Needs: A Guide for Caregivers*. New York: Academic Renewal Press, 2002. Fitchett provides a way to assess the spiritual needs of people.

MacHaffie, Barbara J. *Her Story: Women in Christian Tradition*. Minneapolis: Fortress Press, 2003. MacHaffie's is a well-respected book focusing on the too-often neglected contributions of women in the church generally, including theology.

Pinn, Anne H., and Anthony B. Pinn. *Fortress Introduction to Black Church History*. Minneapolis: Fortress Press, 2002. Black and African American theology are vital ingredients of theological discussion in our time; this book explores that heritage.

Ramsey, Nancy. *Pastoral Diagnosis: A Resource for Ministries of Care and Counseling*. Minneapolis: Fortress Press, 1998. Ramsey suggests a way to do pastoral assessment of parishioners' problems.

Stone, Howard. *Theological Context for Pastoral Caregiving.* New York: Haworth Press, 1996. Provides a theological understanding of the task of ministry—especially pastoral care and counseling ministry.

CHAPTER 4

THEOLOGICAL METHOD

THE DEBATE OVER ABORTION AND REPRODUCTIVE choice. Concern over stem-cell research. A selection from the writings of a medieval theologian. The decision of a terminally ill patient to be allowed to die without heroic measures. The funding of a new Christian education wing to the church. The United States government's policies about refugees. The use of behavior modification in the counseling of children. These, and other such issues, are subjects for theological reflection. Texts, activities, situations, and events outside and within the church also benefit from theological analysis and theological construction.

Since virtually anything is a potential object of theological reflection, how are we to choose what deserves our attention? It would seem fundamental that Christians would want to reflect on their understanding of the Christian message of God. But since their understanding of God's message is worked out in the context of the church, there is also good reason to reflect on the nature of the church. Then again, daily life presents us with many personal, social, and political issues that cannot be avoided. The fact is, we are rarely afforded the leisure to choose what issue upon which to reflect first. More often than not, they hit us in the face.

- Where do you begin?
- How do you proceed?
- How do you develop a theological template?

59

- How do you prioritize the issues of theology in their order of importance?

Issues such as these belong to an area of theology called *theological method,* which examines the bases, proper ordering, and norms of theology. Some theologians specialize in theological method and devote entire books to it. Others—perhaps most of them—alert the reader to their method in the introductory remarks and then go on to present the content of their theology. There are even theologians who simply plunge into their theology without advising anyone of the method being used.

It is not our intention to survey the leading methods current in theology or to propose one as best. Becoming deliberative about theological reflection, however, does involve paying attention to the methods used by other theologians. Conscientious theologians will also want to become clear about the particular theological method they are following.

THE STARTING POINT OF THEOLOGY

Christian theology is reflection on the faith in the Christian message of God in Jesus Christ. The connection between faith and God's message is an invitation to reflect either on the human side of the connection (faith) or on its divine side (God's message).

These two tracks have given rise to a distinction between theologies with an *anthropological or human* starting point and those that begin with *divine revelation.* An anthropological starting point leads theologians to look first at Christian faith in the context of human living and then seek to ascertain the meaning of God's message to the world. Theologies with a revelatory starting point typically begin by focusing on the message of God as revealed in Scripture and/or tradition, only then moving on to explore its human implications.

The question of starting point is a significant one. Where theologians begin influences where their theological reflections will lead them. Each starting point has its merits, but also its risks. An anthropological starting point acknowledges that Christian faith develops within the concrete, specific setting of human life. But anthropologically oriented theologians must be on guard lest their

> Where theologians begin influences where their theological reflections will lead them. Each starting point has its merits, but also its risks.

views become governed more by their personal, social, or cultural milieu than by the distinctiveness of the Christian message.

For its part, a revelatory starting point has the merit of acknowledging that God's message alone determines the character and content of an authentically Christian faith. But theologians working from the sources of revelation need to avoid the very real danger of confusing God's revelation itself with their own fallible grasp of it. The temptation to do so is seductive and perhaps impossible to avoid entirely. They also have to be concerned that in focusing on divine revelation they clearly set forth how it relates to the lives of people in the world of today.

In actual practice, those who go about theological reflection—laypeople, ministers, and academic theologians alike—inevitably take as their starting point who and where they are, here and now. This might be construed as an anthropological starting point except for the fact of who and where Christians are: persons of faith, members of a church, and familiar to some degree with Scripture, tradition, and the language of faith. They have already gathered from their Christian involvements some initial understanding of the meaning of the Christian message.

Starting points include life situations in which Christians find themselves: happy in marriage, worried about their children, hoping for a promotion at work, strapped for money, worried that the politicians have the nation on the wrong track, active in a recycling project. They may feel that they are faithful Christians—less than saintly perhaps, but trying to do the best they can. As church members they attend worship, sing in the choir, bake brownies for the coffee hour, donate time and money to the community hospice. The problems of the outside world infiltrate the church. The congregation seems divided between the members who would like to keep those problems at bay and others who urge responding to them with increased funding and new programs for outreach.

Every one of these matters represents a starting point for theology. They prompt us to reflect on what it means to be faithful to the Christian message of God in these situations. And that involves seeking to understand the meaning of that message.

The starting point for our theology determines where we will go from there, and how we will view even the most seemingly mundane issues theologically. This is illustrated by a controversy that erupted in the council meeting of a suburban Protestant church. The subject under discussion was the adoption of a new hymnal. For years the congregation had been using hymnbooks inherited

> The starting point for our theology determines where we will go from there, and how we will view even the most seemingly mundane issues theologically.

from another church; many people thought the hymns were outdated and all agreed the books were in poor repair.

The denominational loyalists on the council argued, "Christians should stand for something, and if we stand for anything we have to stand up for our church; we can't go on using somebody else's hymns." The opposition retorted, "If we're Christian, people ought to matter more than hymnbooks and any extra money we have should be given to Meals-on-Wheels or some other charity." Another council member argued, "We'll never attract young people when our hymns use sexist language." Finally the budget chair pointed out, "We simply can't afford it." Her dollars-and-cents view won the day, but not the argument. The shouting continued when a council member accused, "All you think about is money," and the budget chair responded, "Christian stewardship means making tough choices; it's a sin to waste money."

Everyone who attended the meeting, or heard about it via the grapevine, had an opinion. Some categorized their views as theological positions; others billed theirs as plain common sense. And there were a few church members on both sides of the issue who observed that "God couldn't care less if we use hymnbooks or not."

The Great Hymnal Controversy is by no means complete as a model of the day-to-day task of theological reflection. Nor is it unique. Tom, for example, had never given much thought to death, let alone a theological view of death and dying, until his mother was diagnosed with terminal cancer three years ago. The term *euthanasia* makes him cringe, bringing to his mind Nazi concentration camps. But last week the doctor said something about withdrawing life support. Tom is overwhelmed; he doesn't know what to think or do. He cannot remember any sermons or church school lessons that addressed terminal illness, except a vague understanding from his early childhood that good people go to heaven when they die. He does recall a visiting speaker during College Week a few years ago who caused quite a row when he commented in passing, "Heaven or Hell, Christianity is for the living, not the dead." One evening Tom looked for the word *cancer* or a synonym in the Bible but couldn't find it.

Tom has been giving a lot of thought to what God wills for his mother. It may not be a good time for him to join a discussion group on theology, but circumstances have forced him to reflect theologically nevertheless. One hopes that he will seek out the counsel of his pastor or a lay friend who has already done some deliberative theological thinking on the issue with which he is struggling. One might also hope that his Christian adviser will know something about cancer, death and dying, life-support systems, and hospital routines as well.

The topics of theological reflection are infinitely varied and, as in Tom's case, ordinarily are chosen for us by our life situation. This is true even of the most scholarly theologies, which often make no mention at all of the real-world setting and proceed in a manner apparently detached from events around them. All theology is context related in the sense that its understanding of faith reflects conditions in the life of the theologian.

CREATIVE THEOLOGY

Whether or not God cares which hymnal a church uses for its Sunday worship, issues like these inevitably come up, every week, in thousands of churches. They can't be wished away; they have to be dealt with. Tom's quandary is less mundane and clearly more urgent. It also cannot be wished away. Whether or not his theology is adequate to the task, he will have to make a decision, and most likely he will ruminate on that decision for the remainder of his life.

It is not difficult to see that when theologians go about thinking, they have to be thinking creatively. Theology is not data crunching. It comes down to issues like Tom's decision about his mother or the Great Hymnal Controversy. We need the facts, to be sure; we also need imagination. We are dealing with meaning, with human need, with our connectedness to God and to one another, with God's intervention in our lives.

In forging an approach to theological reflection that is creative as well as critical, it may be helpful to look at different ways in which our minds deal with information.

Two Modes of Thinking

Sequential thinking is linear cognitive information processing: *A* leads to *B, B* leads to *C*, and so on. Sequential thinking functions logically and analytically. It compares, analyzes, measures, and judges. It orders things successively or chronologically.

Parallel synthetic thinking sees the total picture or *Gestalt* and the interrelatedness of its parts. It processes information all at once, without separately considering each individual factor. It is able to see the interrelationships of a number of factors at the same time without sequentially ordering them. It is adept at the cognitive organization of data that is needed for the perception and interpretation of a painting or photograph. Many bits of data are processed at the same time.

Each of these modes of thinking participates in most activities. They work in partnership to provide the total cognitive functioning of the person. Each mode of cognition has the ability to inhibit the other in order to solve a problem. Our minds switch between

> For theology to be creative, the output of parallel synthetic thinking needs to be integrated with the conceptual constructs of sequential thinking and vice versa.

these two ways of thinking, choosing the most suitable one and inhibiting the other. Sequential thinking and parallel synthetic thinking *complement* each other, but do not replace one another.

Creative thinking involves developing the proficiency of each type of cognition as well as learning to give attention to both modes of thinking.

Most of us have a natural leaning toward either sequential or parallel synthetic thinking. To some extent we may have to live with our inborn tendency; no one's thinking is entirely one way or the other. For theology to be creative, the output of parallel synthetic thinking needs to be integrated with the conceptual constructs of sequential thinking and vice versa. Theological reflection requires both modes of cognitive encoding of data (thinking) for it to be creative.

Creative Thinking

It is possible to create conditions within our environments and schedules, and to structure stages of theological reflection, whereby the fullest possible use is made of both types of cognition (researchers have called this *bilateral cognition*). We refer to the integration of the two modes of thinking as *creative thinking* simply because creativity requires both cognitive approaches. Imagination is play, and it is also discipline. Creativity is inspiration, brought on by research. Creativity is listening and questioning.

Those whose bias is toward parallel synthetic thinking will be able to realize the benefits of sequential cognition by balancing their intuitive style with disciplined scholarship and logical, measurable verification of insights.[1] People involved in day-to-day ministry sometimes fail to give adequate attention to preparation (that is, information gathering and analysis), even dismissing it as a purely head-level operation. As a result, the theological constructs of deliberative theology may have little or no effect on the tasks of ministry; and their pastoral work occurs only out of an embedded theology. These people can do some "pump-priming" activities to enhance the sequential components of their theological reflection. Such activities may include daily readings in Scripture and theology that actively work toward the continued development of a deliberative theology.

Another sequential task that some Christians neglect is verification. In this connection, the sequential mode of thinking can be fostered by the simple method of putting one's insights into written form. (There is a reason professors require so many written papers:

> Deliberative theological reflection is a communal task; verification requires sharing our thoughts with others.

writing helps to clarify one's thinking.) The experiences of ministry are indeed raw material for theological formulation, but only if the Christian as theologian takes the time—if necessary, scheduled and rigorously observed—to articulate and test insights gained from that experience. Verification is further enhanced through sharing our reflected insights—through preaching, teaching, and writing—with others who might profit from them. It is engaging in theological conversation. Deliberative theological reflection is a communal task; verification requires sharing our thoughts with others.

Similarly, individuals who find themselves more prone to sequential modes of information processing need to stop the incessant analyzing that can stifle imagination and impede understanding. They need to be receptive to insights that come to them while they are not overtly working on a specific problem, and to trust and nurture these discoveries.

Listening to music, playing the piano, gardening, meditating, walking or jogging, painting, or even such mindless undertakings as folding the Sunday bulletin or washing the car, can allow parallel thinking to occur. Spiritual disciplines also benefit the intuitive thought processes so necessary to theological reflection. Structuring one's schedule to include a number of pump-priming activities of parallel synthetic cognition will enrich our creative thinking.

The *ah-ha* can arrive in a variety of forms—a visual image, a sudden recollection, a burst of ideas. In a pastoral visit it may appear as a childhood memory, a parable, or a story from Scripture bubbling to the surface of consciousness. Whenever it comes, we need to recognize it, seize it, listen to it, use it.

Reflection that is theological reflection is creative. It relies upon both sequential and parallel synthetic cognitive processing. Christians as theologians at times have to enhance their abilities for creative thinking by doing pump-priming activities. Theological reflection is an imaginative, craftlike enterprise.

A RUDIMENTARY PROCEDURE

Theological reflection is a creative process. It pays attention to where we begin—the starting point. The question remains, *How do we begin?* What is involved as we go about the task of deliberative theological reflection upon the Great Hymnal Controversy or the decision regarding life support for a dying parent or any other issue that confronts us? Is there a procedure the council members could have used to make their deliberations smoother and—more important—enriching to their faith? Are there some basic elements Tom can get a grasp on, to give him a sense of order in his confusion?

This much, at least, is called for as we deliberate theologically on the questions and struggles of our Christian lives:

- to make explicit the theological understandings of the Christian message implicit in the discussion;
- to examine those understandings and note their strengths and limits;
- to propose what seems the most adequate resolution to the issue in light of the Christian message of God; and
- to explain in theological terms why what we propose is preferable to other options.

The first two tasks are primarily functions of *theological analysis,* which is the investigative side of theological method that sets out to discover the understanding of faith implicit or explicit within any issue. The latter two tasks fall under the heading of *theological construction,* which strives to interpret matters in light of the Christian message. Both tasks are essential in creative deliberative theological reflection, and in practice are interrelated and carried out together.

There was no list of church council discussion topics from which the Great Hymnal Controversy was selected. Nor did Tom pick the subject of artificial life support for his dying mother from a menu of life crises calling for theological reflection. To repeat: The subjects for our theological reflection have a tendency to choose themselves. Given that, we need to know what to look for in the theologies of others, or in responding to real-life issues in our own lives, that will help us approach our theological reflection in an orderly and not haphazard fashion.

The following three chapters will propose three sets of diagnostic exercises—questions, really—that can serve as the basis of a procedure for doing theological reflection and will facilitate the analytical and constructive theological tasks. The first set looks at the issue in light of the *gospel*; the second in terms of the *human condition*; and the third diagnostic set examines the implications of *Christian vocation* as they bear on the matter at hand.

Each question in turn (though not necessarily in order) can be applied to every issue that calls for our theological deliberation. The exercises surely will not cover all that could be said about the meaning of the Christian message of God. But they strike near the very heart of the concerns of Christian faith. In exploring these questions, something is disclosed of the breadth and depth of the Christian message. They provide a staging area for later, more complete, reflection.

None of these tasks or exercises is to be thought of as a rigid rule for the theological enterprise. They are, instead, guides. They can help us through the fractious chaos of a skirmish in congregational affairs or the bewildering chaos of a life-or-death decision. A theological method can bring some order to that chaos—not order for its own sake, but for the confidence that our views and actions are in keeping with our Christian faith. They make it possible for the Christian message of God to have an impact upon the mundane as well as the crucial matters of our lives.

For Further Reading

Saliers, Don E. *Worship as Theology: Foretaste of Glory Divine.* Nashville: Abingdon Press, 1994. Saliers, one of today's most theologically insightful writers on worship, explores the God-centered and human-oriented dimensions of Christian worship.

Thistlethwaite, Susan Brooks, and Mary Potter Engel. *Lift Every Voice: Constructing Christian Theologies from the Underside.* Revised and expanded edition. Maryknoll, N.Y.: Orbis Books, 1998. A multinational, multiethnic, multiracial, and otherwise diverse list of distinguished contributors discuss their current thinking on classic Christian doctrines and issues.

White, James F. *A Brief History of Christian Worship.* Nashville: Abingdon Press, 1993. Much of Christian theology arises from worship and is most at home there. White's is a classic survey of worship in Christianity's major church traditions.

Wilson-Dickson, Andrew. *The Story of Christian Music.* Minneapolis: Fortress Press; Oxford: Lion Publishing, 2003. Christians in every congregation can put their own theology and church practices of music and hymn-singing in proper historical and cultural context, thanks to this wide-ranging overview of church music.

CHAPTER 5

THE GOSPEL

YOU HAVE LOST YOUR JOB WITH LITTLE CHANCE OF finding another position in your field; you struggle to redefine yourself and your place in the world.

Your widowed mother is making increasing demands on your time and money, and it is putting stress on your marriage.

The pastor needs a raise, everyone agrees, but, since people are unlikely to give more to the church, that raise will have to be taken out of benevolences.

A council member of the inner-city church has taken it upon himself to place a prominent sign at the edge of its lot that reads: "Private Property—Keep Out."

Thousands in a warring African nation are dying of starvation and disease, but relief workers have resources to help only one in ten.

In the Great Hymnal Controversy members have a choice: go ahead and buy the new hymnals, with inclusive language and songs from many cultures, or just get by with the old ones and give the money to a world hunger organization.

There is a congressional election in your district. As a voter, you have to choose between a seasoned incumbent with whose views you do not completely agree but who has the political savvy to get things done, or an idealistic young candidate who has a brilliant agenda of changes to make America better but may not be very effective at achieving them.

The natural, immediate response to life situations such as these is to ask, What do you do? It is a vital, necessary question that cannot be put off for long (see chap. 7). But for Christians there is a prior question that requires an answer, one that will shape what we do. It is at the heart of the faith: What is the gospel in this dilemma? Not, What do we do, but, *What does the gospel mean here?* Reflecting on the meaning of gospel, we will see, means articulating our basic faith commitments.

DIAGNOSTIC EXERCISE ONE

How we view life's crises and dilemmas, how we reflect upon them theologically, and what choices we make in that light depend upon our understanding of the gospel—God's good news in Jesus Christ. The gospel is the touchstone for Christians; it is the core of meaning behind their faith, behind what they do and what happens to them. For this reason, the first diagnostic exercise to aid us in the task of reflecting theologically on any of these issues addresses the *meaning of the gospel* itself as it is brought to bear upon the matter

> The gospel is the touchstone for Christians; it is the core of meaning behind their faith, behind what they do and what happens to them.

at hand. Three questions lend themselves to theological reflection on the gospel:

- What is the gospel?
- How does the gospel reach people?
- How do people receive the gospel and its benefits?

Each question opens up a line of inquiry to be pursued in theological reflection.

What Is the Gospel?

Gospel is among many words used by Christians to speak of the essentials of the Christian message of God. In ordinary Greek it referred to a public announcement of glad tidings, such as the news of a birth in a royal family, a victory in war, or a treaty of peace. Christians used the term for the preaching and teaching of their faith. They were making a public announcement that God's message was glad tidings to all the world. Their references to the gospel attest that the announcement concerns Jesus.

The letters of Paul contain several very early summaries of the content of this message. He reminds the church at Corinth, for example, of the gospel he received and passed on to them, that Christ died for our sins according to the Scriptures, that he was buried, and that he was raised on the third day according to the Scriptures (1 Cor. 15:3). To the church at Rome, Paul writes of the gospel of God "concerning his Son, who was descended from David according to the flesh and was declared to be Son of God with power according to the spirit of holiness by resurrection from the dead, Jesus Christ our Lord, through whom we have received grace" (Rom. 1:3-5).

Many similar formulations of the gospel message appear elsewhere in the New Testament and other early Christian writings. The use of the word *gospel* in the titles of books such as Matthew, Mark, Luke, and John shows that the early church also set forth the meaning of God's message by retelling the story of the life, death, and resurrection of Jesus Christ.

The conviction that Jesus was of decisive theological significance distinguished newly emergent Christianity from other faith communities. Through Christ, the early Christians claimed, the purpose of God for humanity and all of creation is made known. In the New Testament this purpose is referred to as salvation, the love of God, the forgiveness of sins, the coming of the reign of God, the grace of God, and covenant. Christians have used these and many other shorthand terms to point to the meaning of the good news. Varied as they are, all point to a life-changing event that has taken place.

Theological reflection on the gospel frequently focuses on questions concerning its content. The summary statements of Paul mention a few things about Jesus; the four Gospels tell a great deal more. We might ask, Since so many terms have been used to describe the transformation brought about by the gospel, how can they be fashioned together to make a coherent overall picture?

Why, for example, do Paul and other Christian theologians say that the death of Christ took place "for our sins"? Can we explain why the story of Jesus is said to change our lives and to mark a turning point in the course of human history?

Another line of theological reflection, pursued in order to clarify the meaning of the gospel, compares the "goodness" of the gospel for human history with the sorry state of things apart

> New Testament references to law and gospel reveal the concern of early Christians to define their identity in relationship to the heritage of Judaism.

from this message. In speaking of Jesus as the light of the world, for example, the Gospel of John plays on the contrast between the darkness of night and the brightness of day. Many other contrasts are made by biblical and later theological writers: those who are dead in sin receive new life; the condemned are pardoned; slaves are made free; aliens become citizens; those lost are found; evil is overcome by righteousness; despair gives way to hope. Many different images are used to portray the meaning of the gospel.

One recurrent approach to examining the meaning of the gospel is to discuss it in terms of its relationship to the notion of *law*. Matthew depicts the gospel of God as the law of God, which is rightly interpreted by Jesus. In Matthew's view, then, the primary task of faithful disciples is obedience to the law of Christ. Paul conveys another view: he describes the gospel as both the fulfillment and the end of the law. New Testament references to law and gospel reveal the concern of early Christians to define their identity in relationship to the heritage of Judaism.

The relationship between law and gospel became a much-contested question during the Reformation era. These disputes had to do less with Jewish law in particular than with the various good works of obedience taught by the church. For Luther, law and gospel are the two sides of the Christian message of God. Law sets forth what God commands humans to be and do; gospel sets forth what God promises to be and do for those who, having failed to observe the commands perfectly, stand condemned by the law. Luther repeatedly warned against confusing law and gospel. For example, those who preach that the gospel means to love God and one's neighbor rather than God's promise of unconditional love and merciful acceptance (justification) of sinners in Jesus Christ are interpreting gospel as law.

The lines of reflection suggested here are not the only ones that theologians could pursue. The point of the first question of this exercise—What is the gospel?—is that coming to an understanding of the gospel's meaning is a bottom-line issue for every Christian theologian. Have we received any good news we can count on? Can we share it with others? What role does Jesus of Nazareth play in the gospel message? How are we to describe the effects and benefits of the gospel? Identifying what a theologian says about these matters helps us determine what he or she really stands for. To clarify our own understanding of what the gospel means is to move toward a truly deliberative theology.

How Does the Gospel Reach People?

The figure of Jesus is understood to be the means by which God makes known glad tidings to the world. Thus, early Christians referred not only to the gospel but to the gospel of Jesus Christ, and not only to salvation but to salvation in Jesus Christ. References to other means by which the gospel is made known are understood to be derived from what God has done in Jesus Christ. The earthly life of Jesus was brief. Once the generation that had known him passed away, knowledge of the gospel would die unless it was passed on by other means.

The church understood—and still understands—itself to be that means. Its proclamation of the gospel continues the ministry

> Lest the church forget or distort the gospel, it has a duty constantly to search the Scriptures, rely on them, live in conformity to them, and test its practice by them.

of Jesus and makes God's good news known to all nations. So the church is a means by which God continues to impart the good news to people.

The church also understands its Scriptures to be a means by which the gospel is announced. Here a written record of the story of God's will and action toward the world is available. Lest the church forget or distort the gospel, it has a duty constantly to search the Scriptures, rely on them, live in conformity to them, and test its practice by them.

It is not the Scriptures alone but the whole life of the church that is to preserve and communicate the gospel. Worship, rituals, sacraments, activities in the outside world are to be means by which the gospel is communicated. Therefore, whether the church is making known the gospel and not some other message is one of theology's chief concerns.

It may seem obvious to Christians that the church's task is to embody and communicate the gospel. This task is entrusted to the church as a gift and an obligation coming from God. Such statements, however, raise many serious issues that deliberative theologians have to address. Is it the case, for example, that God's good news to the world is made known only in Jesus Christ or is the will of God revealed by other means as well, by other persons and at other times and places? When speaking of the church as the means by which the gospel comes to the world, is it true that outside the church there is no salvation? Is it not the case that the church is as sinful as it is saintly and therefore that God's promise of salvation can come to pass even if churches prove weak or faithless? How can Christians proclaim the gospel confidently without seeming smug or arrogant? Issues such as these certainly require theological attention.

The point of the second question of this diagnostic exercise is that theologians cannot content themselves with speaking of the gospel as though it exists only in the Bible, or floats through the atmosphere like the ultraviolet rays of the sun. The gospel is a treasure *carried* "in clay jars," as Paul put it. It is up to theologians to explain how the gospel is conveyed. Thus, inquiring Christians will want to know: By what means does this theology understand the gospel to be made known to the world?

For the church council debating the purchase of new hymnals, a clearer understanding of the church's role in promulgating the gospel might have facilitated the discussion. Tom, who is already searching the Scriptures on his own for help in dealing with his mother's imminent death, might be prompted to seek more help from the church: as a companion to the Scripture in making the gospel of Jesus known and as a potential source of guidance and strength in making his hard decision regarding life-support removal.

How Do People Receive the Gospel and Its Benefits?

Announcements elicit responses. They are welcomed or ignored. The gospel is an announcement that things are no longer as they

> Faith does not mean merely assenting to certain phrases. It means viewing our own lives and everything else in light of the gospel.

were, that something of life-transforming significance has happened. Our responses to the announcement are crucial. To reject or to ignore this message is to set ourselves at odds with God. The good news has been heard, but it has had no impact. We take no comfort in it and gain no hope from it.

Theologians often have suggested that delighting in the beneficial effects of God's good news calls for acknowledging that this news is God's and that it is good. This response is referred to as *faith*—believing and trusting in the gospel, accepting and confessing Jesus Christ. Faith does not mean merely assenting to certain phrases. It means viewing our own lives and everything else in light of the gospel. It means committing ourselves to live ever-mindful of the love of God in Jesus Christ. Understanding faith—how people embrace the gospel—is a critical part of theology.

The man who came to Jesus and asked what he had to do in order to inherit eternal life was posing this third question (Mark 10:17; Luke 18:18; cf. Matt. 19:16). What response did the gospel required of him? Having affirmed that he had kept the law since birth, the man was told that the one thing remaining was to sell all that he owned and give it to the poor. Why this one thing? Is the point, as many Christians have said, to extend and intensify the law beyond its customary reach? Or is it that the gospel confronts the man with the one thing that he had not done and could not do of his own will, thereby demonstrating the futility of every human attempt to calculate how much work is necessary for salvation?

The criminal on the cross next to Jesus was asking this question as well, but he expected little for himself. His life was over;

what could he do? He asked only that Jesus remember him, and he received this assurance: "Today you will be with me in Paradise" (Luke 23:43). In a sense, his question was itself a response. Recognizing (though perhaps not fully understanding) who Jesus was, he made a humble request that could be viewed as an offering of what little life or hope he had left.

To receive the gospel and enjoy its benefits is to let Jesus come into your heart, make a public confession of faith, receive the Lord's Supper, be baptized, be "born again," do penance, give generously, participate in the fellowship, mortify the flesh, forgive your enemies, struggle for justice, strive for holiness, make peace, obey church teachings. All this, and much, much more, has been cited at one time or another in Christians' discussions of how people can come to receive the benefits of the gospel.

Such a listing is only suggestive of the sort of answers that can be given to this basic question—How do people receive the gospel and its benefits? Your first reaction to these items deserves to be taken seriously. Is what you have always considered essential missing? Is too much being required of Christians? Would you not say, for example, that all those who are baptized and partake of Holy Communion receive something of the benefits of the gospel even though their strivings for holiness are feeble indeed? Perhaps it would be better to call all of these things opportunities rather than requirements. Perhaps not.

In any case, it takes only a moment's thought to remind us how important it is for theologians to be clear about how people come to share in the benefits of the gospel. The task of theology requires that we make judgments about claims—ours and those of others—concerning how God's message in Jesus Christ becomes a vital force in the lives of people today.

THE CASE OF THE TRIMBLES

Yolanda and DeWayne Trimble were enthusiastic about teaching the church school in October. Since joining the couples class last year they had enjoyed getting to know others their age who were starting families, had dual careers, and were devoted to the church.

They also enjoyed what the class called its open format. Instead of relying on a regular lecturer or a formal lesson plan, each couple took its turn as coteachers once each month. Some weeks were better than others. The different speakers on a variety of topics made the class interesting.

Yolanda and DeWayne worked up a joint presentation called "refinding yourself." It was based on a book they had come across a year earlier, which told of gaining peace and well-being by "refinding your innermost self, the unconscious wellspring for love of life." This, the author had pointed out, was the fundamental aim of all the great teachings of religion and philosophy throughout history and the chief concern of medical science, psychology, and social science today.

Observing the book's seven overlooked clues to one's innermost self had helped Yolanda and DeWayne through a difficult period in their marriage. DeWayne now took work pressures more in stride, gave up his evening cocktails, and devoted the weekends to their children. Yolanda gained energy by losing weight and getting in shape. The time-management recommendations opened up for her precious moments of relaxation, refreshment, and community involvement. Their new lease on life was something they wanted to share with the class.

The Trimbles' presentation began by pointing out that the Bible says Jesus came so that people would live life abundantly. Then they spoke of the seven clues for "refinding" the innermost self and of the good that can come from doing so. At the end, they shared how, through the process of refinding their selves, they had rededicated themselves to church. At the benediction of each worship service DeWayne and Yolanda join hands as a couple and give thanks for how God has blessed them.

SUGGESTIONS FOR THEOLOGICAL ANALYSIS

Initial responses to this church-school lesson will surely vary according to people's life situations and embedded theologies. Some class members may be eager to buy the book and do as the

Trimbles have done. There may be those who wish the church would deal more with family living in such practical and helpful terms. Others may doubt that a turnaround in life is really so simple—or that it can happen at all. They may even feel envious or resentful, thinking that success like that of the Trimbles is beyond them. The living-happily-ever-after-in-suburbia ending may put some off. Still others will seriously question whether the clues to refinding the self have anything to do with the Christian religion. After all, mention was made of God, Jesus Christ, and the church only briefly at the beginning and end of the lesson. Surely some will add that it seems unduly harsh to reproach the couple, since the book has been of value to them and might be for others.

Amid the mix of responses, what can be said about the content of the message of *good news* brought by DeWayne and Yolanda? How does it reach people? How do they come to receive it and its benefits?

The Trimbles certainly announced a message of good news. Its content was a "love of life abundant." It was presented as a possibility for all who earnestly seek it. This message, they proposed, reaches people through listening about the truth of our innermost self and following various suggestions for refinding it. The message and its benefits are received by changing our thinking and our acting in the suggested ways.

Even simple comparison of this "good news" with that spoken of in Scripture and tradition prompts a number of questions for us as theologians: In what way does the story of Jesus Christ relate to the content of this message? What role does the community of faith—its Scriptures, worship, sacraments, and social life—play in the bringing of this news? How do the suggestions, the clues for refinding our self, square with Christian testimonies about the path that leads to the life of faith? Is the so-called innermost self what Christian theology terms the human soul or spirit? Is "love of life" indeed the same basic message communicated by the life, death, and resurrection of Jesus Christ?

In answering such questions, theologians should not be too hasty. It is not clear whether this message is intended to be a substitute for or a restatement of the Christian gospel. The Trimbles believe that the author of the book is correct—that the thrust of the message is the same as the one found in the teachings of Jesus. In their view, what the Bible calls "life abundant" and what the book calls "love of life" basically mean the same thing. They view the seven clues as spiritual disciplines to be followed at home along with other religious practices carried out in the context of the church. The Trimbles have integrated the two in such a way that it does not even occur to them that, strictly speaking, neither Jesus Christ, the Christian faith, nor the church are essential to the program of refinding one's innermost self.

A deliberative theologian will not let the matter rest here but will evaluate the source and content of the message in light of the Christian message of God. Study of the teachings of Jesus and the biblical phrase "life abundant" is called for. Do they support the view of the self-help program the Trimbles are sharing? And what of other essential themes in the Scriptures—the notion, for example, that the path of discipleship is "the way of the cross"? How does this tally with the gospel of peaceful living through "refinding yourself"? Likewise, one must study the spiritual disciplines of Scripture and church history in order to determine whether the seven clues are merely helpful additions, or outright competitors, to Christian practice. (Thoughtful theologians will also want to examine whether this particular notion of the "innermost self" has any solid basis in psychological theory and clinical practice.)

Above all, this message needs to be evaluated in terms of what it says about the character of the relationship between God and humanity. Although the Trimbles thank God for having blessed

> It is critical to establish one's own theological account of what the gospel is, how it is imparted, and how we receive its benefits.

them, the gospel of refinding our innermost selves in itself does not require that they do so. Nor does it speak of God's purposes or God's grace. (These topics lead to a second diagnostic exercise, focusing on the human condition. We will cover that exercise in the next chapter.)

Other questions could and should be asked of any self-avowed theological statement, whether it appears in a liturgy, a church newsletter, the words of a counselee, or a self-help book on refinding yourself. Above all, it is critical to establish one's own theological account of what the gospel is, how it is imparted, and how we receive its benefits. To do so is to set out on a journey of deliberative theology and will serve as a foundation for all further theological work.

For Further Reading

Farley, Edward. *Practicing Gospel: Unconventional Thoughts on the Church's Ministry.* Louisville: Westminster John Knox Press, 2003. Farley holds theology and the practices of ministry together, indicating that the gospel does have an impact on what we do as Christians and ministers.

Pelikan, Jaroslav. *Jesus through the Centuries.* New Haven: Yale University Press, 1999. A premier historian of Christian doctrine, Pelikan surveys a collection of diverse verbal and visual "pictures" of Jesus from biblical times to today.

CHAPTER 6

THE HUMAN CONDITION

ONE VERSION OF THE PUBLIC CONFESSION THAT IS repeated each Sunday in many Christian churches begins: "We confess that we are in bondage to sin and cannot free ourselves. We have sinned against you in thought, word, and deed. We have not loved you with our whole heart, we have not loved our neighbors as ourselves."

This, of course, is a liturgical confession of sin and not a complete account of the human condition. But it brings to our minds aspects of that condition that we would perhaps rather ignore as we go about our daily lives. How we understand our condition as humans—not only our strengths and our preciousness to God, but also our limits and our opposition to God—is an important part of how we reflect theologically on the circumstances and events of our lives. The second diagnostic exercise, therefore, addresses the condition in which humans find themselves. (Chronologically it may occur first, since who and where we are is the starting point for all of our theologizing.) It also deals with the difference that the gospel makes in our lives and with the way in which this change comes about.

DIAGNOSTIC EXERCISE TWO

These are the concerns of Christian anthropology—that is, the very theological understanding of the human person. Three questions advance our theological reflection on the human condition:

- What is the basic problem with the human condition? (What is sin?)
- What is the resolution to that problem in the human condition? (What is salvation?)
- How is the problem resolved? (What is the means of salvation?)

Clearly, these are value-laden, not altogether neutral, questions. They concern themselves with limits and possibilities, and they distinguish between human life as it is and as it could become. They fix our sights on matters of long-standing concern to Christian theologians.

Two cautions are in order at the outset. First, the two parts of each question are interdependent, each requiring consideration of the other. Thus, in references to the human condition, attention has to be directed to sin, and vice versa.

Second, in doing this exercise it is important to move back and forth between particulars and abstract generalities. For example, the word *sin* has been used sometimes in a very concrete sense and at other times in a broad way. (This will be discussed in more detail as part of the first question, below.) Particularity versus generality is also an issue in references made to the human condition.

Few people, apart from philosophers and some literary commentators, speak in a sweeping sense of the Human Condition. They deal with the specifics of their own condition, in tangible and individualized terms. The teenager who seeks counseling for drug addiction is not likely to bring up the problem of the human condition in so many words. Neither do speakers at community meetings called to deal with neighborhood crime and police brutality. A keen sense of the individuality of each person and situation raises healthy suspicions about universalistic statements concerning the human condition.

Nevertheless, there is reason to wonder whether this suspicion about overgeneralization might be carried too far. The novels of Maya Angelou, the poems of Sylvia Plath, the works of Euripides and Dostoyevsky refer to the life stories of their characters with utter specificity. Yet the characters' problems and attempts to resolve them may well cast light on the reader's own human condition. They can offer food for theological reflection. The stories of Adam and Eve, Moses, Miriam, Peter, Thomas, Mary Magdalene, and Paul—and Jesus!—also shed light on how things stand between God and human beings.

Sweeping comments about human finitude, fallibility, moral weakness, and the like do arise when people are confronted with their compulsive behavior. Carlos, for example, had only one reply to his wife and friends who tried to talk to him about his gambling problem: "Well, I'm only human." He implied that gamblers, like all people, are limited, fallible individuals, which somehow excuses their self-destructive behavior. Neither implication is inherently true. Deliberative reflection requires that we relate such generalized views of human nature to the particularities of individual situations.

With those two cautions in mind, we proceed to the three questions of the exercise.

What Is the Basic Problem with the Human Condition? (What Is Sin?)

Some human problems seem to defy resolution. Ancient Greek tragedies cast common experiences into dramas about the limits of human existence: a problem unfolds, and, despite every human attempt to overcome it, the outcome is fated. Oedipus the king, wise and good, sets out to solve the mystery of his father's murder and unwittingly brings disaster upon himself and others. Aristotle praised tragedies for their cathartic effect: they helped their audience come to terms with the limits of their human condition.

The classical literary counterpoint to tragedy is comedy, a story that is not necessarily humorous but that comes to a happy end. The comedic (optimistic) interpretation of the human condition is often expressed in today's many self-help books. It also underlies modern society's pervasive faith in technological solutions to human problems. Successful movie stars proclaim that "You can be whatever you want to be." The TV news reports a scientist's opinion that human population growth will never outstrip the earth's resources because of fast-developing advances in fertilizers or hydroponics or, if all else fails, the colonization of outer space.

It is the task of deliberative theological reflection to discern the implicit understanding of the human condition beneath these and similar claims. What view of the human condition resides within a young man who, at age five, saw his father murder his mother and then commit suicide, at age eight walked into his brother's room to find him dead from a drug overdose, and from that time on bounced from foster home to foster home, by sixteen a diagnosed schizophrenic with little hope in a world that seems unremittingly cruel? Must this young man's problems be attributed to his sin, or perhaps that of his parents? Have society's sinful shortcomings led to this terrible result? Was it the result of the fall? The answers to such questions will never be fixed once and for all but can serve as a foundation for theological reflection on the human condition.

What comes into view when our human condition is seen from the perspective of the Christian message of God? Scripture records that human beings were created by God. It also records that sin is

> *Sin* refers to specific behaviors, to the status or character of people, and to a single and pervasive problem (being at odds with God's purposes).

always a factor in human life. But the word *sin* is used in differing ways throughout the Bible and in theology. Theologians strive to be clear about the meaning of the term. For example, *sin* refers to specific behaviors, to the status or character of people, and to a single and pervasive problem (being at odds with God's purposes). Violations of God's commandments (specific behaviors) are called *sins*. In a more general sense, such violations taken together comprise our *sin*, which makes each of us a sinner. Finally, *sinfulness* is a condition rather than an infraction. It is said that all are born in sin and the world is lost in sin. The condition of all humanity is to be at odds with God.

Attempts to clarify the relationship between sins, sin, and sinfulness have led to some of the most provocative and disputed issues of theology. Both Scripture and tradition record debates that turn on whether humans are sinners because they have violated some specific divine law, or they commit sins because they are sinners. The doctrines of original sin, the fall, and human depravity press the point still further—suggesting that sinfulness has become in some sense an inescapable feature of human life. These views have been criticized as pessimistic, unappreciative of God's goodness and justice, and inconsistent with human freedom and accountability. Even so, they cast light on some of the most baffling experiences of the Christian life. There is, for example, the experience of being at such odds with God's will that we are no longer capable of confessing, like Paul, that "the good that I would do, I do not do."

Understanding sin is a challenge for all who do theological reflection. One reason for the difficulty is that there never has been an agreed-upon listing of the many attitudes and actions that are called sins. In ancient Israel, for example, it was considered a sin for a man whose brother died to refuse to marry his brother's widow. In Shakespeare's time, as *Hamlet* tells us, such a marriage was considered sinfully incestuous. Today, few Christians would attach the word *sin* to such a marriage, one way or the other. The important thing, they are likely to say, is whether the marriage is based on a truly voluntary, loving, and committed relationship between the two partners.

This illustration reminds us that acts viewed as sins in one particular cultural milieu or social setting may not be thought of that way in another. It is up to theologians to decide which commands and prohibitions are of enduring validity and which should be left to pass with the changing times. Both an obligation to care for family and a prohibition against incestuous marriages have endured within Judaism and Christianity. What has altered over time is how these obligations relate to changing, culturally accepted views of the biological, legal, and moral relationships that constitute family membership. Some theologians attempt to deal with such questions by defining sin in ever-greater detail. Others, however, are inclined to define sin more broadly—as doing something harmful to others, for example—so that the term is applicable in a wide range of circumstances.

The human condition is so multifaceted and complex that no single concept is adequate to describe it. A multiplicity of terms must be used in order to capture its full meaning. A clear sense of the range of meaning conveyed by sins, sin, and sinfulness is an integral part of theological reflection.

What Is the Resolution to the Problem of the Human Condition? (What Is Salvation?)

People have problems, some of them serious—that is the human condition. Word that our problems can be resolved comes as good news. From a Christian perspective, perhaps the most basic of all

Christian theologians often have argued that the true character of the human condition can only be grasped by way of contrast to God's message of salvation that comes in Jesus Christ.

our problems is how to live in proper relationship to God, others, and creation.

Christian theologians often have argued that the true character of the human condition can only be grasped by way of contrast to God's message of salvation that comes in Jesus Christ. Salvation connotes health, wholeness, and rescue. It is only one of a number of images Christians commonly use when speaking of the decisive changes brought about by the gospel. Among the others are forgiveness, blessing, redemption, reconciliation, justification, sanctification, new life, and life abundant.

Since the beginning, Christians have spoken of salvation as a tension: already present, yet awaiting completion. The Lord's Supper, for example, is referred to as a foretaste of the heavenly banquet yet to come. The Christian life is said to be marked at once by freedom and joy in the present and hope for the future. As dramas of salvation are played out over the course of history, the temptation to separate its present from its future reality occasionally proves hard to resist; some theologies are emphatically this-worldly, and others just as emphatically otherworldly.

Christian soteriology (the doctrine or study of salvation) attempts to distinguish the role of God's action and human action in the reality of salvation. Few theologians would deny that salvation is a gift of God, or assert that human beings save themselves. Nevertheless, some of them stress that salvation is only God's work, while others detect in such views a failure to consider any human participation. Is grace unconditional and irresistible? Or is it an offer that humans are free to accept or reject? Is the kingdom of God brought in by God's direct intervention, or do human efforts help build it here on earth?

How Is the Problem Resolved? (What Is the Means of Salvation?)

The salvation that Christians proclaim has always been associated with the person and work of Jesus. He, it is said, is the way, the truth, and the life. The special status of Jesus is that of *Savior*. It is the task of the branch of theology called Christology to develop a proper doctrine of the work and person of Christ.

But in early Christianity "the Way" referred not only to Jesus but to the life of the church. The Way is the path followed by faithful disciples of Christ who continue his ministry by proclaiming the gospel of salvation. Preaching and the sacraments, as proclamations of this message, are the means of grace. Precisely how God's grace is conveyed by these means is the concern of ecclesiology (the doctrine of the church).

Is membership in the church itself a means of grace? The phrase *extra ecclesiam nulla salus est* ("outside the church there is no salvation") has been repeated through generations of Christian theology. Is it true that there is no salvation outside the institution of the church? What about Christians who are by circumstances isolated from other Christians? In what respects is the Way of Christian people synonymous with God's Way?

Theological reflection is needed. Whatever answers are occasioned by that reflection will have a bearing on the specific issues Christians confront. If, for example, the church is viewed as the sole or primary means of grace, the church council members who opposed buying new hymnbooks might do well to look carefully at the wording of the hymns in the old books before casting their final ballots. In his dilemma Tom might be led to encircle himself and his mother with not only the support but also the guidance (or even the authority) of the church.

SIN, SALVATION, AND THE HUMAN CONDITION

Views of such central matters as sin, salvation, and how sinners are saved do not appear in splendid isolation in theology; they are inextricably related to each other. Unfortunately, in the church and in Christian life the connections between them can be vague and ill defined. For example, a pastor may preach a sermon about sin on the Third Sunday of Advent that has no discernible ties with the following week's sermon on feeding the hungry, and both seem unrelated to the Christmas Eve sermon about the Incarnation. In short, worshipers are left to cope with apparently random messages unless the minister has helped the congregation to draw the relationships that are necessary for a coherent system of meanings.

A bare-bones summary of historical theological classifications of sin, salvation, and the means of grace might provide insight into the problem of relating these themes. Christian views of *sin* seem to fall into four clusters, in which sin is viewed primarily as ignorance, corruptible mortality, broken relationship or alienation, and bondage or oppression. There are also four corresponding clusters of theological themes regarding *salvation*: bringing true knowledge, incorruptible immortality, reconciliation (justification), and freedom. Finally, there are four parallel theological clusters concerning the *means of salvation,* in which Jesus is viewed as the teacher of wisdom, the victor over death, the Crucified and Risen One who restores a right relationship with God, and the Liberator.

This typology is by necessity an oversimplification, but its images appear repeatedly in the history of theology, as well as in

> Christians who seek to formulate an adequate view of sin, salvation, and how sinners are saved are duty-bound to take seriously the diversity of Christian language.

Scripture. It is rare indeed to find any extended theological statement that uses only one of the clusters to the total exclusion of the others. This suggests that the problem of the human condition is so multifaceted that Christians are not content without combining these themes of faith.

This mixing of symbols contributes to the richness of the language of prayer and worship, but it can also lead to confused church members. Christians who seek to formulate an adequate view of sin, salvation, and how sinners are saved are duty-bound to take seriously the diversity of Christian language, noting when multiple views of these matters do not completely agree but offer different shades of meaning.

THE CASE OF THE GREAT
PEASANTS' WAR

The peasants living in Germany at the time of the Reformation suffered pervasive economic and social misery. Crime, disease, hunger, oppression, and early death had long been their plight. Sporadic, localized rebellions against the rich and powerful were not unusual. One such uprising began in the summer of 1524 in the area of the Black Forest. The disturbances quickly spread, and this bitter conflict has come to be known as the Great Peasants' War.

Its scope and intensity distinguished the Great Peasants' War from previous rebellions. Another distinctive mark was the widespread use of slogans (for instance, the true gospel, Christian freedom, Scripture alone, and the priesthood of all believers) associated with Martin Luther's call for church reform. The war itself, however, was not an attempt to establish Lutheranism. The most famous list of peasant demands, the Twelve Articles of 1525, focused primarily on economic concerns—permission to fish and hunt and cut timber, adjustment of rents, the reduction of taxes and tithes to the church, and the proper administration of justice. The peasants also insisted that each local community be allowed to choose its own pastor and that, "since Christ redeemed us all with the shedding of his precious blood," serfs should be freed. The Twelve Articles explained that "the basis of all the articles" was a desire to live in accord with the gospel, a just Christian demand that only "certain antichristians and enemies of the gospel" oppose and seek to suppress.[1]

Luther initially responded as a mediator. He professed sympathy with the lot of the peasants and criticized the nobility for its callous disregard of their reasonable demands. He also admonished the peasants for taking the law into their own hands and committing acts of violence against persons and property. But as the revolt became (in his eyes) more excessive and anarchistic, he lashed out in a tract "Against the Murderous and Thieving Rabble of the Peasants," calling upon the nobility to use force to quell the rebels. The nobles hardly needed Luther's advice. They were already at work on a counteroffensive when the tract was published. In a brief time the revolt was put down.

SUGGESTIONS FOR THEOLOGICAL REFLECTION

The European feudal system of lords and peasantry has long since passed away. Even so, the instinct to take sides is hard to quell. The particularities of this long-gone event seem less important than its symbolic meaning. The peasants stand either for the down-trodden of the world or for all who resort to violence in order to improve their lot. The nobles, likewise, represent either oppressors or defenders of law and order. And Luther stands for the church and each of its members who must decide which side they will take in times of economic and political upheaval.

Historians may urge us to take a dispassionate, evenhanded view of the conflict, yet Christians in every century since the peasants' revolt find that they cannot resist second-guessing Luther. Some conclude that his response is a blot on the church's record; others believe that it was a shame, but he did what had to be done; and still others conclude that he should have taken a stronger stand against anarchy and rebellion.

Despite the differences between sixteenth-century Germany and the economic and political systems of the twenty-first century, a number of the theological points at issue during Luther's years are still with us. It is no easier dealing with them today. The apostle Paul believed political authorities were ordained by God, and Christians had a duty to obey them. What that means in terms of a wide range of systems of governments from democratic to despotic is far from obvious. In America, church and state are not linked as in sixteenth-century Germany, when the peasants accused their (nominally) Christian rulers of being anti-Christians and enemies of the gospel. Although insisting that everything be done in accord with the Word of God, the peasants did not seek to establish democracy or grant religious liberty to everyone. Now, as then, Christians can agree that their faith calls them to work for peace but disagree over whether the use of violent force is ever justified in bringing about peace.

In responding to this case study, it is wise to separate the various issues that are involved. Among the most important are those addressed by the diagnostic exercise focusing on the human condition—a Christian understanding of sin, salvation, and the means of salvation. Theological reflection along these lines cannot be boiled down to a simple pro or con response to sixteenth-century events. It may be aided by learning more about that era, and the

> Christians can agree that their faith calls them to work for peace but disagree over whether the use of violent force is ever justified in bringing about peace.

thinking of the peasants and Luther in particular. The issues themselves are perennial, however, and cannot be responsibly answered by reference to the historical sources alone.

A deliberative theologian presses to the fundamental understanding of faith at play in this specific incident before deciding on the symbolic meaning it holds for Christian living today. The vision of the peasants should not be trivialized. Even though the cutting of timber on common lands was one of their demands, one would miss the point to say that they viewed the problem with the human condition to be just a lack of timber, and its true resolution (salvation) merely the availability of more timber. No doubt a favorable response to such a demand would have been welcome to them and may have restored calm—at least for a time. The peasants' key theological concern would still remain. For the peasants, the fundamental problem of the human condition was the control over God's creation by rulers who, lacking faith and violating the truth of the Word, made common cause with the powers of evil and oppression. The resolution of this problem would be the reinstatement of the rule of justice and freedom in accord with God's purpose for the world. This end would be achieved by the exposure of the unjust stewards, appeals for renewed commitment to Christian teachings, and finally the forcible overthrow of the oppressors—as God freed the children of Israel from the hand of Pharaoh.

Several issues should be considered in Luther's response to the rebellion. In spite of sympathy for the plight of the peasants and criticism of unjust, hard-hearted nobles, Luther denied that robbery, murder, and destruction were justified by appeal to the gospel. He rejected the view that Christian liberty means release from physical burdens. He upheld the command to be obedient to secular authorities and sharply distinguished between "the two kingdoms"—the kingdom of the world and the kingdom of God. Each of these issues is a theological matter in its own right. Indeed, thoughtful interpreters of Luther have frequently pointed to apparent internal inconsistencies in his consideration of the relationship of religion and politics.

Throughout it all, however, Luther operated with a different appraisal of the human condition than that expressed in the writings of defense of the rebellion. To Luther, the basic problem with the human condition (including the issues in the Great Peasants' Way) was sin, which he viewed primarily as a broken relationship with God. Created to live in right relationship with God and with one another, humans had instead turned from their Creator in search of autonomy. Like the prodigal son, having alienated themselves from the One who gave them life, they proceeded to do all manner of evil. Luther held that the only resolution to this estrangement is the grace of God—that is, God's forgiveness and acceptance of us despite our sin. This rescue is accomplished through the giving of the law and the sending of the Savior, Jesus Christ. Although the law serves to restrain evildoers and limit some of the damage that we humans inflict upon one another, it primarily serves to drive us toward Christ. Even our best efforts to keep the law reveal that we fall hopelessly short of sinless perfection. Everything we do, as Luther wrote, is "tainted with sin." No alternative is left except to confess our sinfulness and place ourselves at the mercy of God.

Each of the two differing views of the human condition that surface in this case finds support both in Scripture and tradition. Reasoned arguments may be advanced in favor of both. The experience of Christians would seem to indicate, on the one hand, that a Luther-like view of the human condition, focusing on sin as a broken relationship with God, has all too often been used by the well-to-do to defend their privileges. On the other hand, the peasant-like view of sin as injustice or oppression has all too often been used to justify replacing one set of unjust rulers with another. Neither outcome was what the peasants or Luther really favored.

Had the issues been discussed in a sixteenth-century think tank, those upholding the views of the peasants might concede that, though their cause was righteous, their means involved regrettably evil deeds. Those taking the views of Luther might concede that, just as one good turn deserves another, so the evil of sinful overlords can be expected to incite their sinful subjects to evil. Nevertheless, differences between the two parties would be hard to bridge. Luther would have to insist that just deeds alone— of nobles or peasants—cannot resolve the basic problem with the human condition. That resolution comes to pass solely by the grace of God. The peasants would have to insist that whatever else the grace of God may mean, it must involve a decisive reordering of human relations toward greater justice and freedom.

Of course, differing views of the human condition do not by themselves fully explain why the peasants rebelled or Luther came to act as he did in this particular situation. It is even possible for a deliberative theologian to agree with the peasants' position on the human condition and yet refuse to condone mass rebellion and anarchy, or to agree with Luther and yet seek the overthrow of oppressive principalities and powers. Whatever the action that Christians understand their faith calls them to undertake, it is to be intricately related to their views of the human condition.

For Further Reading

Birch, Bruce C., and Larry L. Rasmussen. *The Bible and Ethics in the Christian Life.* Revised and expanded edition. Minneapolis: Augsburg, 1988. Biblical references to sin (and its synonyms) are so many and varied that one is well advised to survey the forest before deciding on hugging or cutting down any one particular tree. Birch and Rasmussen do not pretend to answer Christian moral dilemmas, but they provide perspective, and much insight, for thoughtful Christians.

Ray, Stephen G., Jr. *Do No Harm: Social Sin and Christian Responsibility.* Minneapolis: Fortress Press, 2003. Luther's response to the Peasants' Revolt remains a still much-disputed issue; it raises a perennial theological concern regarding "the human condition" and Christian responses to it. Ray's book is an informative and thought-provoking work on the social dimension of sins, sin, and sinfulness.

CHAPTER 7

VOCATION

ALL CHRISTIANS ARE CALLED BY GOD . . . BUT *TO WHAT*
are we called? Where are we asked to be? What are we called to
do? Christians understand themselves to be called by God—called
to be truly Christian, faithful witnesses to the gospel of God in
Jesus Christ. The theological term for this responsibility is *vocation*. It refers to the call to be faithful in the immediate context of
one's life, including one's social station (age, gender, marital status, race, ethnic heritage, economic status, abilities), one's work
(homemaker, farmer, teacher, laborer, technician, health worker,
performer), one's geography (Asian, European, African, urban,
rural, desert, mountain), and last but certainly not least, one's participation in the overall ministry of the church (Eastern Orthodox,
Roman Catholic, or some branch of Protestantism).

In an attempt to understand the meaning of faith, Christian
theology invariably concerns itself with questions of vocation. Yet
there is no single heading for it in the literature of theology, such as
"the doctrine of Christian action." Christian vocation covers a wide
and ever-spreading range of concerns. Technological advances and
the complexities of modern life daily lead us into new territory as
we strive to reflect theologically on our role and our behavior as
Christians in the world.

From a theological standpoint, the question of Christian
action can only be asked from the perspective of a proper understanding of faith as expressed in the gospel message, announcing

97

that God has taken life-transforming and world-changing action in the person of Jesus.

This announcement calls for a human response of faith and calls forth the creation of a community of the faithful, the church. Theologians have emphasized that the life of faith is itself a calling: the church and its members are summoned to live in the world as faithful witnesses to the will of God. The community of faith has a God-given mission (from the Latin *missio,* to send forth) and each of its members a God-given vocation (from the Latin *vocare,* to summon or call). They fulfill this calling by the lives they lead. A

> The Christian vocation includes those actions that are undertaken jointly by the community of faith as a whole as well as those carried out by its members individually.

key task of theology, therefore, is to describe the meaning of Christian calling.

Taken in its broadest sense, the Christian vocation includes those actions that are undertaken jointly by the community of faith as a whole as well as those carried out by its members individually. This mix of corporate and individual vocation figures in historical theological conversations and in contemporary, day-to-day, congregational discussions.

In theological accounts of the nature of the church, the church's calling is typically described in such broad headings as proclamation of the faith by word and deed, worship and sacraments, the upbuilding of the community of faith, acts of service, reconciliation, and justice and peacemaking.

The vocation of each individual Christian is likewise manifold. It involves contributing to the church's efforts to fulfill its mission. It includes acting as a Christian amid the particularities of daily involvement in the world. This dimension of Christian vocation was given special attention in the theological writings of the sixteenth-century reformers—especially Martin Luther—and has since become widely acknowledged in Protestantism and beyond. Although special services like ordained ministry, religious orders, and missionary activities are high and noble callings, *all* Christians are summoned to be faithful servants of God in the context of their life situation. Whatever their age, gender, marital status, ethnicity, health, occupation, social roles, or talents, Christians are to serve God in all that they do.

In a recent regional church newspaper we came across a wide array of (perhaps embedded) theological views concerning what Christians are called upon to do. Here are some excerpts from that single publication:

- "God has called Christians to be occupied in good works. . . . That is, in the midst of your academic activity you have separate time to gather in church as the children of God."
- "Maybe that is what's troubling our beloved church these days. We have somehow forgotten that if others are to see the face of Jesus, we who call ourselves his followers must learn his characteristics intimately so that our faces openly proclaim his message."
- "I came to the point where I said if Christianity is true, then this is a call to a radically different lifestyle and worldview. . . . Because I am a Christian I do the best I can to be fair and accurate in my reporting and I set my personal biases aside."
- "The language of bigots and racists, regardless of race, religion or ethnic background, contradicts the basic principles of each of our faiths and cannot be met with silence."
- "Our call for renewed commitment to common witness . . . is not a call for one more thing to be done in our churches; it is a call to be faithful to the very essence of our Christian identity. God has always called God's people to be active and engaged in finding new ways to serve God's cause and God's church."

Other views beyond number might be added to these, for Christians devote a great deal of energy, thought, and conversation to their vocations. Their voices are not always harmonious, but the question clearly is important to them. And, as the snippets from the denominational newspaper illustrate, such comments often are cast in ethical terms and convey a sense of moral obligation. This is by no means surprising. "What is the right thing to do?" is a question that faces every individual or community. Answering the question involves taking into account not only the situation itself but also the moral views that people bring to it. Christians often make reference to Christian or un-Christian behavior. In so doing, they interpret the situations they encounter with a conscious or implicit ethical system.

But asking, "How are *Christians* called upon to act?" implies that being Christian calls forth actions that may not be in agreement with other-than-Christian standards. It also implies that there are Christian-specific reasons for acting and Christian-specific criteria for deciding which actions are in keeping with the will of God. The history of Christianity shows that neither churches nor all their members have agreed upon any single definition of these Christian-specific factors, although all of them commonly assume that, however understood, they are of decisive importance for the Christian life. Committed Christians understand themselves to be under obligation to uphold certain values and to undertake some actions while opposing others.

So it is that the question, "What are Christians called upon to do?" is an inescapable consideration for the church. It comes into play as Christians go about deciding what to do in every situation they face.

DIAGNOSTIC EXERCISE THREE

It would be vain to promise that doing a diagnostic exercise on Christian vocation will lead church members to become better, more faithful Christians. After all, it is one thing to reflect on what faith calls us to do and quite another to follow through on that call. For that, Scripture and tradition recommend a renewal and increase of faith empowered by the Spirit. But theological reflection can serve to clarify and guide our actions as we seek to live the Christian life.

Three questions lend themselves to reflecting theologically on Christian vocation.

- What deeds are Christians called to do?
- What are the reasons for performing a service or action?
- Why is one course of action the most fitting in a given situation?

A few comments are in order before beginning the third exercise. First, like the others, this one is designed to strike near the heart of theology's concerns—in this case, theological concerns about Christian action. At the same time, the open-ended questions permit dealing with a wide variety of situations. The exercise is only a quick study and should ultimately lead to more comprehensive theological reflection.

Second, service, deeds, and actions are used synonymously. One might just as properly use the word *ministry,* since the root meaning of ministry is service. "Service" bridges talk of human action and talk of Christian ministry. Although everyone acts, Christian theological reflection concerns itself especially with how Christians are called to act. These actions are viewed, from a theological standpoint, as the outgrowth of Christian faith in God's message to the world. They are the means by which Christians serve God and the neighbor and in so doing undertake the ministry to which they are called.

What Deeds Are Christians Called to Do?

Every real-life situation is an occasion for theological reflection. What is a Christian called to do, for example, when a colleague at work makes a racial slur, a homeless person interrupts a church meeting with a request for a handout, the nightly news reports famine in another land, an "adult bookstore" opens up near the high school, the coming election includes a referendum on parimutuel betting, or rumors fly that the pastor is having an extramarital affair?

These and countless situations like them come up in the course of church life. People in the church express their views about how Christians ought to respond to whatever is going on in the world. This diagnostic question can be applied to the situations themselves, and also to laws, rules, and directives made by others.

Scripture beckons Christians to be the people of God, a light to the nations, whose words and deeds make the will of God known to all the world. This vocation involves remembering all that God has done. It also involves a commitment to demonstrate what it means to pray "Thy will be done on earth, as it is in heaven."

From earliest times Christian communities have understood their calling to be at once a gift to be received with gratitude and a duty to be undertaken. Christians have interpreted this calling in a variety of ways. Christian people are called, for example, to worship, baptize, celebrate the Lord's Supper, upbuild the church, pray ceaselessly, love the Lord their God with all their heart, mind, and

From earliest times Christian communities have understood their calling to be at once a gift to be received with gratitude and a duty to be undertaken.

soul and their neighbor as themselves, forgive those who persecute them, renounce the devil, resist evil, seek justice, and much more.

As varied and even conflictive as these biddings are, they represent for Christians ways of being faithful to their calling. Discriminating the most appropriate understanding of Christian service from among the different views found in both Scripture and tradition has been a matter of ongoing controversy in the church. Cultural values find their way into Christian views of their calling so unconsciously that at times it is difficult to distinguish what is Christian from what are simply societal norms.

The theological heritage of various denominations transmits a certain understanding of what Christians are called upon to do, as well as certain standards for evaluating their actions. There is no denying that in the church there is always talk—even heated debate—about how Christians ought to act. Church members regularly differ on the standards for Christian action, praising or condemning others for their views. Heated arguments break out when the church cannot speak in one voice or act in concert because of divergent understandings of Christian vocation. Such controversies are especially painful in churches; after all, Christians have been instructed to act in ways that promote unity, peace, and loving accord.

The God-given calling of Christians, however it may be defined, is not just something to believe in but a task to be undertaken. It is carried out in the context of specific situations—at home or at work, in social and cultural affairs. Theological reflection requires Christians continually to consider what actions they are called upon to take.

What Are the Reasons for Performing a Service or Action?

This second question of the diagnostic exercise on Christian vocation examines *why* any action is to be regarded as the *Christian* thing to do. Although people often seem to act out of mere habit, ethical analysis reveals that human behavior is by its very nature motivated and purposive. Ordinary conversation points this out: "What do you think you're doing?" "Why did you say that?" "What possessed you to do that?" When someone tries to make us stop doing something or even suggest a course of action, we are likely to ask why. (We started doing so at about the age of two!) Efforts at persuasion are always calculated to give some rationale for the request even if it be no more than the last resort of a frustrated parent: "Because I said so."

Experience suggests that the reasons for our action are at times hard to pin down. They are so deeply rooted in us, so subtle or complex, that we are hard-pressed to get at them. Not only that; the reasons we cite for our actions occasionally sound (even to ourselves) like lame excuses or rationalizations. And the reasons others give as they try to persuade us to do a particular action may sound contrived. Even so, having and being given reasons for human actions are part and parcel of living.

Theological reflection on the reasons for commending a course of action must deal with at least three concerns. It seeks first to uncover the real reasons behind the action in question. Second, it attempts, from all reasons given for a particular action, to separate out the distinctly *Christian* reasons. And third, it examines whether the reasons given are sufficient to justify a particular action. After all, an earnest attempt to be faithful to our Christian calling does not necessarily mean that any given deed is the one and only faithful action to be taken.

In short, we ask:

- What are the *real* reasons?
- What are the *Christian* reasons?
- Are they *sufficient* reasons?

Throughout the history of the church the reasons Christians have given for the actions they take typically combine "because-of" reasons and "in-order-to" reasons. Christian *because-of* reasons make reference to some premise in the Christian message that leads to the suggested action. Thus it is said, for example, that we are called to love others because Christ first loved us. Or we are called to work for peace because Jesus said, "Blessed are the peacemakers." Or we are asked to lobby the state legislature to end subsidies to parochial schools because our denomination insisted on a strict separation of church and state.

Christian *in-order-to* reasons, on the other hand, make reference to some goal or outcome that Christians believe is important. Thus Christians might be heard to say that the church should support the plan to send United Nations peacekeepers into some region of bloodshed in order to bring about the harmony that God

> Throughout the history of the church the reasons Christians have given for the actions they take typically combine "because-of" reasons and "in-order-to" reasons.

wills for all people. Or it might be said that Christians should give generously to the church's day-care center in order to provide all needy children with a safe and wholesome environment during the after-school hours.

Why Is One Course of Action the Most Fitting in a Given Situation?

Having examined reasons for various courses of action, we find that most issues which call for theological reflection (like the Great Hymnal Controversy, Tom's tragic dilemma, and countless others) require that we choose one action or service to the exclusion of all others. The third question of the exercise on vocation deals with the appropriateness of that one exclusive choice.

Let us begin with a case study. A homeless person walked in on the worship committee meeting at St. Andrew's Church one Wednesday night and asked for help. The church organist jumped up from her chair and quickly ushered the man out, pressing a five-dollar bill in his hand. At the break, one committee member remarked to the organist, "That was a stupid thing to do—he'll go buy liquor with that money." A lively discussion arose as various people aired their views of what the organist should have done. "We have a church charity fund—you should have told him to come back later and talk to the minister," said one. "He needed directions to the community welfare office—they could help him out," said another. "You shouldn't have kicked him out like that— we could have all prayed together with him," said yet a third. The organist, half hurt and half angry, could only say, "I was just trying to help him—that's what a Christian is supposed to do, isn't it?"

It seems only fair to grant that one of the reasons why the organist responded as she did included her sense of Christian obligation to help a person in need—and at the same time to get on with the business at hand. The incident happened so quickly and her action was so spontaneous that her sense of Christian obligation functioned almost automatically—and unreflectively. It flowed out of her embedded theology.

The justification the organist offered for her action also arose from her embedded theology. The idea that being helpful to a homeless person is the Christian thing to do was, in her view, something everyone present would agree on. What if she had said, "I hate people like that so much that I'd do anything to get rid of them" or "Planning worship is more important than wasting time with deadbeats"? Surely neither the action nor its justification would have passed muster with her fellow Christians.

How fitting was the five-dollar gift? The organist chose her action out of a range of several morally acceptable actions. The worship-committee members had no quarrel with the morality of her choice; it was the *appropriateness* of the handout that they questioned.

Determining the suitability of an action takes into consideration both the reasons for doing it and the situation. Two lines of examination, then, need to be pursued. We examine first *whether* Christian vocation can be rightly expressed in this particular situation. Then, assuming that it can, we seek to discover what action is the most appropriate to the situation.

There have always been Christians who hold that the suitability of certain actions needs no further examination. Deliberative theological reflection about fittingness may question moral standards that have already been decided by the church.

Why examine the questions of ordaining women to the ministry when Jesus chose only men as his twelve disciples? Why examine whether it is fitting for Christians to have images in their churches now that the iconoclast controversies of the Byzantine church and its flare-ups in the early days of the Reformation have simmered down?

It is hard at times to come up with Christian reasons for reopening cases that have been settled. Indeed, there are some, who might be called moral absolutists, who hold that God's rules for living are fixed for all time. Behind that view is the conviction that faithfulness to the Christian calling is already stipulated by biblical or churchly guidelines that are obligatory in every situation. Under no circumstances whatsoever are Christians to, let us say, practice sorcery or tell a lie or commit murder or engage in military conflict. But even moral absolutists are bound to their circumstances. They view the world, and read the language of the Bible, with the assumptions and preconceptions of their own time and culture. Take the moral proscription against lying, for one example. On one hand, telling the factual truth can be highly inappropriate—meddlesome and harmful to others—as when a third party spills marital secrets. On the other hand, we have all witnessed cases of prevarication by people who "would never tell a lie" and yet, by their misuse of factual statements, led others to believe a falsehood or put an inaccurate gloss on a situation.

In most cases, Christians must figure out the most fitting way to act faithfully by applying Christian sensibilities to the specific, complex, and often difficult situations in which they find themselves. This does not mean that the Christian thing to do is optional; it means only that decisions about the Christian thing to do *involve genuine theological deliberation* rather than following an already fully prescribed rule. Even the best-known guidelines for faithful living, such as the Ten Commandments and the golden rule, must be interpreted and applied in light of changing situations. How they are to be interpreted calls for theological reflection.

Differences over such decisions are often at the heart of church conflicts. Paul faced opponents who insisted that, however otherwise loving they were to one another, Jewish and Gentile Christians should not eat together. In the Middle Ages, the Roman Catholic

Church came to the view that vows of poverty and chastity were not incumbent on all Christians but were "counsels of perfection"

> In most cases, Christians must figure out the most fitting way to act faithfully by applying Christian sensibilities to the specific, complex, and often difficult situations in which they find themselves.

that only exceptionally dedicated laypersons and ordained priests were called to follow. In the 1940s, the German theologian Dietrich Bonhoeffer concluded after much soul-searching that, despite the biblical prohibition of murder and the admonition to obey political authorities, it was not only right but fitting to join in a conspiracy to assassinate Adolf Hitler.

The point of the third question of the diagnostic exercise on Christian vocation is to choose one particular view or action that is the most fitting expression of Christian faithfulness in a given situation. Let us return to the incident at the worship-committee meeting. Assuming that all of the coffee-break commentators were, like the church organist, concerned to do the Christian thing for Christian reasons, their remarks lead us to wonder whether the organist's action was the most fitting one that might have been taken.

From the information we have, it is impossible to judge whether any of the committee members thought the organist's action was wrong or un-Christian. The harshest remark—that what she did was "stupid"—may have been a code word implying that some other action would have been more fitting. Those who spoke up obviously preferred other options. It seemed to them more fitting, for example, to send the homeless person to see the minister or a social worker at the community welfare center.

Faced with questions about the most fitting response to the homeless man's request, the organist's explanation of trying to be helpful was sincere but a little too general to adequately account for the aptness of her deed. The homeless man may have known he would be interrupting a meeting in progress and counted on being bribed out the door with a few dollars; what if they had surprised him—engaged him in conversation, or offered some active rather than passive assistance? There is at least a possibility that the less-expected response would have been a chance for real ministry to him. That opportunity was lost in the knee-jerk (though well-intentioned) action of the organist.

In the real world, a Christian sense of calling rarely demands that we act in only one particular manner. It leads instead to a certain range of options, any of which might be undertaken morally and responsibly. The question then remains: Which is the most fitting? And often it remains as a conundrum because uncertainties

> In the real world, a Christian sense of calling rarely demands that we act in only one particular manner. It leads instead to a certain range of options, any of which might be undertaken morally and responsibly.

or disagreements can arise at so many points: views of Christian calling, views of Christian reasons for various actions, or views of the actual situation.

It is not possible for theological reflection to resolve all such conflicts. But by examining the ways an action can be deemed the most fitting service for Christians, theologically reflective Christians perform a ministry that might otherwise go undone. They help unravel the threads of conviction that are woven into difficult moral choices. They help not only themselves but the entire body of Christ arrive at decisions concerning how Christians ought to act.

THE CASE OF A CHURCH'S MINISTRY TO HOMELESS PERSONS

Two years after a homeless person interrupted the worship-committee meeting at First Church, the local newspaper ran a feature article with the headline "From Homelessness to Hopefulness: At First Church, Christian Caring Counts." It opened with an interview with Sarah, who told how members at First Church helped her escape from the streets, move into a small but safe apartment of her own, and become an active member of the congregation. The report then described the community outreach program to the homeless that First Church had launched and the new hope it brought to Sarah and others like her.

The article went on to say that the growing number of the homeless in First Church's neighborhood had concerned many in the congregation. Deciding on such a program took a great deal of prayer and hard work, and while many obstacles had been overcome, many challenges still remained. Testimonials from the pastor, laypersons, and Sarah herself confirmed that regardless of its difficulties, it was truly a worthwhile ministry.

The program was a new venture for First Church. Having resolved to do something to minister to the many homeless who were around the church, the congregation had learned much. They had become aware of the people in the church's own neighborhood, the housing problem, the bureaucracy of social-service agencies, and grassroots politics. Many of the volunteer "friends" of the homeless became street-smart and came to realize that friendliness meant perseverance and tough love rather than pity or condescension. They made contact with social-service agencies, the housing authority, and numerous civic organizations. Two other churches, one of them a storefront ministry, joined in the effort. As a result, a few of the many people living on the street had been helped to find low-cost housing, receive benefits from governmental programs, and begin to rebuild their lives. Sarah was one of those helped by First Church.

Although the newspaper focused on the positive aspects of Sarah's story, establishing a ministry for the homeless was not without difficulties. Obstacles to the program included a stormy debate within the church and the community about even having an outreach program, confrontations with representatives of various public agencies, and the disheartening realization that only a small number of the homeless responded to the help offered. Sarah was the exception, not the rule. Her fall through the social net had not been as hard as it had been for others. She had inner strength and untapped resources that, once given a chance, landed her back on her feet.

What the article called "the challenges ahead" included the question of whether First Church should continue to invest so much time and energy in the program, given the meager gains that were being realized. First Church also had to decide whether it was prepared to welcome into its membership more of the homeless, especially those less responsive than Sarah. Indeed, there already were complaints from neighbors that the churches' so-called ministry to the homeless was attracting too many unde-sirables into the area.

SUGGESTIONS FOR THEOLOGICAL REFLECTION

In undertaking the program for the homeless, First Church worked its way through the questions of the third diagnostic exercise on vocation without ever being aware of it. Members of First Church had long taken for granted (by tradition) that as Christians they were called to preach the gospel and celebrate the sacraments, pro-vide for church school education, join in fellowship, and serve the community. Little thought had been given, however, to responding to the plight of the homeless—except to tell those who asked for aid where to find the community welfare office and to provide the pastor with a charity fund.

The incident two years before at the worship-committee meeting might have ended there. But when the story of what hap-pened was mentioned at the church's board meeting, it led to lively discussion and numerous suggestions for reaching out and offer-ing help to the homeless. Resistance to such an outreach ministry ("the pastor does enough already, we don't have time or money for that") forced others to make their embedded theologies explicit. Christ, they said, came to serve the poor, the outcast, the needy, and those who follow him are called to do the same.

Those who favored an outreach ministry did not automatically win the day. In the course of time their proposals prevailed, in large part because a ministry to the homeless provided one answer to the first two critical questions of the diagnostic exercise on Chris-tian vocation. No one was prepared to argue that "as Christians, our faith calls us to do nothing at all." The key justification cited by advocates of a ministry to the homeless was a *because-of* reason: an appeal to the basic image of the Christian life as discipleship in keeping with the model of Christlike living. Although some mem-bers of the congregation had worries about carrying these ideas too far, they could not argue with its merit.

Other reasons might also have been offered from Scripture and tradition, and from the life experiences of parishioners who could speak of the pain they felt when the church had seemed indifferent to them in times of distress. Had the debate continued, appeals of this sort are likely to have been made.

It would have been helpful if *in-order-to* reasons also had been raised. At the time, it did not seem necessary to clarify the objectives or outcome of the ministry. General agreement on caring seemed sufficient, even though some church members agreed to the ministry on the unspoken assumption that it would win the homeless to Christ, others thought it would contribute to social justice, and still others believed that such an outreach program might strengthen families and help restore law and order in the neighborhood.

The failure to reflect on what it means, in practice, to care for others did not become evident until the church tried to decide what was the most fitting action to be taken. Only then did this lapse in the congregation's theological deliberations begin to cause new problems.

First, the proposed program for the homeless was what most members described as moderate, attempting no direct confrontation with either the systemic sociopolitical conditions that can spawn homelessness or the spiritual-moral roots of self-destructive behavior among some of the homeless themselves. By focusing on friendship as well as social service, there was both an individual and a social dimension to the problem of homelessness. Most at the church saw its calling neither as redeeming the homeless from bondage to evil nor as reforming city government.

Second, precisely because the objectives of the ministry were not clear, the church volunteers had difficulty figuring out when they were being helpful and when they were being used. They were uncertain when to cooperate with and when to resist local government or neighbors who might oppose what they were doing. Everyone agreed that Sarah was certainly a success story; but the continuation of the program hinged on reasoned judgments about the effectiveness of what was being done in light of study and experience.

What is the most fitting response of Christians? First Church made a stab at answering that question. It is fitting for Christians to serve those in need, as Christ himself had done. It is fitting for that service to involve offering friendship and opportunity for improved living conditions. It is fitting to demonstrate the meaning of God's good news and invite the homeless to respond to it. It is fitting to work with—perhaps at times to "finesse"—the powers that be, but not contest their authority. All this is woven in the fabric of the theological understanding of Christian vocation in First Church's ministry.

The members of First Church now face a new question: Is what they first considered fitting for Christians truly the most appropriate response, given their understanding of vocation and the particularities of the situation? They need to anchor their worthy aims to clear and specific objectives. They need to examine their ministry to the homeless in relation to their other ministries—such as evangelism, worship, church school, overseas missions—and decide where they should give their greatest effort. These questions call for ongoing theological deliberation and a clarified understanding of their Christian vocation. Answering *all* three questions of this diagnostic exercise are necessary for First Church to determine how they are to fulfill their Christian vocation.

FOR FURTHER READING

Benne, Robert. *Ordinary Saints: An Introduction to the Christian Life.* Second edition. Minneapolis: Fortress Press, 2003. The meaning of faithfulness is a theological matter, and Benne provides a study guide along with his own constructive thinking on the Christian identity and vocation (calling).

Gustafson, James M. *An Examined Faith: The Grace of Self-Doubt.* Minneapolis: Fortress Press, 2004. Gustafson, a foremost Reformed tradition scholar, reflects on the conflicts that Christians face when they are unclear about how their language of faith and doctrine relates to—and differs from—interpretations of issues and events that are commonplace in science, politics, the media, and much of today's "religious disputes."

Volf, Miroslav, and Dorothy C. Bass, eds. *Practicing Theology: Beliefs and Practices in Christian Life.* Grand Rapids, Mich.: Eerdmans, 2002. Thirteen theological scholars, men and women of diverse backgrounds, offer reflections on theology as "beliefs and practices" in daily living.

CHAPTER 8

THEOLOGICAL REFLECTION IN CHRISTIAN COMMUNITY

OUR GIFTS DIFFER. A PAINTER WHO CAN CREATE A large canvas with skill, beauty, and insight may have little interest or aptitude in the technical requirements of the photographic arts. A stonemason who cuts and fits together huge blocks of stone with precision may find it hard to thread a needle, much less sew a fine garment.

In the same way, the craft of theological reflection depends to some extent on natural aptitudes. Virtually everyone has gifts for theological reflection, though their gifts may differ. Some people are more adept at one aspect of the task than at others. For example, a person may be masterful at examining the writings of other theologians but almost at a loss when it comes to making a theological response to a counseling relationship or a social issue.

For every Christian struggling to do theology in spite of an apparent lack of natural talents, however, surely there are scores who are underusing the gifts they do have. Seriousness of purpose, persistence, and practice go a long way to make up for any initial weakness. One of our hopes for this book is that it will enable readers to expand and enrich their competencies for the task.

The diagnostic exercises described in the preceding chapters were devised to facilitate this growth in theological reflection. The comments and specific suggestions offered in this and the final chapter aim at raising the comfort level for the task and placing theological reflection in the context where it occurs—critical thinking, spiritual formation, the community of faith, and day-to-day life in the trenches of human existence.

CRITICAL THEOLOGY

At its best, theological reflection is attentive to the testimony of the Scriptures and receptive to the promptings of the Spirit. At its best, it is also *critical inquiry*. That is not to say it is negative or faultfinding, but it questions. It takes an honest, observant, probing stance toward everything that falls under the watchful eye of the Christian as theologian. The theologian sees things in a different light by asking and answering question after question. New insights into the ongoing work of God are gained.

Embedded theologies express answers about the meaning of the Christian message of God that are already inherent in the church and the experience of its members. Deliberative theology is an additive step. It reflects on those answers and the situation out of which they arise, and poses the primary question: Do these answers adequately convey the meaning of the Christian message for the people of faith?

This primary question turns theological reflection into critical inquiry, for it challenges (at least temporarily) every status quo understanding of faith. The critical questions raised in quest of a deliberative theology are of the sort that thoughtful Christians ask because they are called to seek a more satisfactory understanding of the faith. They are exploratory questions. Critical inquirers want to know: Is this understanding of Christian faith adequate? If so,

> The critical questions raised in quest of a deliberative theology are of the sort that thoughtful Christians ask because they are called to seek a more satisfactory understanding of the faith.

why? If not, why not? Can a revised, more adequate understanding be developed?

The approach to critical inquiry in theology described in this book has similarities to models of critical thinking in other fields of study—for example, the disciplines of music, literature, and art criticism. The process is not arbitrary or even original. It is an orderly and organic approach that rarely proceeds in a one-two-three chronological fashion. The elements of critical thinking are interrelated and frequently overlap. They include description, analysis, framing a view, judgment, and response.

Description

To describe is to give a clearheaded look at the subject of theological reflection. The subject of that reflection is the *situation* (for instance, the Great Hymnal Controversy, Tom's mother's impending death, Luther and the peasants' revolt) and the *embedded theology* that is brought to that situation. Accurately describing every observable aspect and detail of the situation, the problem, or the topic and detecting the embedded theology is a first step toward dealing with it in an honest critical light—"Just the facts, ma'am." The journalistic questions "who, what, where, and when" are a good beginning for such description.

Accurate description is as necessary for clear thinking in theological reflection as it is in any endeavor. If we have lurched ahead into a knee-jerk response or a dead-end analysis based on incomplete information, it is always possible to back up, step aside, and gather more information.

Sometimes it is helpful to write down the results of our careful observation, and, in fact, readers who are serious about their theological enterprise might do well to keep a journal for that purpose. The act of putting our observations on paper often stimulates and clarifies our thinking. Reading over the description may remind us of information we have missed and provide insight and an overview that might not be possible with more casual observations.

Questioning helps us to observe accurately. Going back to the case of the organist's handout, for example: Is the worship committee running behind or is it ahead of schedule with its agenda? How many times has this same homeless man visited the church on the Wednesday meeting nights? What is the condition of his voice? His complexion? What does he say he will do with the money? Has the church established a policy for dealing with requests such as his? If so, what is that policy? What is the theology that motivated the organist's gift? What were the embedded theological understandings of the other members of the worship committee who proposed other responses than giving him money? A quick mental description of the situation could have answered most of these questions in a matter of minutes.

Or, in Tom's dilemma: What, according to the doctor, is the prognosis for Tom's mother? Is she conscious? Can she express her wishes? What is her theological understanding of euthanasia and death? What is the family's theology of death and life? Does she have a living will? If they withdraw life support, how much longer is she likely to live? What will happen if she does not die right away? Will she suffer? If life support is continued, is there any shred of hope for recovery? Will drugs ease her pain? If so, will they leave her so diminished that her life is virtually over anyway?

Who is available to help with Tom's decision process? Is there a chaplain at the hospital? Has Tom's pastor encountered similar situations in her ministry? What happened in those cases? Are there other family members whose input would be helpful, or would they only make it more difficult for Tom?

And so on. Sometimes we question what is patently obvious. Some of the details we observe may be irrelevant. But in the stress of a crisis or an argument or a time of need, we are likely to miss much pertinent data. Thus, observation, guided by accurate description, is vital for accurate critical theological reflection.

Analysis

Such critical questioning drives the ongoing conversation that makes up the history of theology. The analysis phase of critical theological thinking devotes itself to deeper, more probing questions.

The task of critical inquiry in Western Christianity during the twentieth century has focused on three main lines of questioning. The first, a by-product of modern philosophy and science, is the test by *reason and experience*. It asks, for example, how God could be one and yet three, as the doctrine of the Trinity claims. How can a belief in biblical or postbiblical miracles be squared with a sound scientific account of the laws of nature?

A second line of questioning has its roots in the rise of historical consciousness and modern approaches to the study of *history*.

The variability of Christian views is taken seriously. How, for example, can the truths of faith be said to be unchanging when history shows that Christian teaching has changed over time? Does research confirm the historical accuracy of the biblical narratives? What forces of history shaped the belief, practice, and organization of the churches and, in light of those influences, which features of Christianity deserve to be called God-given or permanent and judged worthy of continuing despite changing times?

A third line of analytical questioning has as its focus *the conditions of human living*—the psychological, sociological, economic, and political forces that shape the course of human life. Theologians have sought to come to grips with the social issues of their times. What, if anything, does belief in the soul have to do with DNA research, fetal transplants, or abortion? Does Christianity commend the American version of the nuclear family, or does it include other forms of loving, committed relationships? If there is any truth to the theological claim that in Christ "there is no longer Jew or Greek, there is no longer slave or free, there is no longer male and female" (Gal. 3:28), how can churches promote evangelistic programs leading to monoethnic, monocultural, and class-bound congregations?

The effects of critical analysis along this third line are evident in much contemporary theological discussion. Inquiring Christians want to know: What does theology have to say about such matters as poverty, world hunger, ecology, welfare, gender issues, racial and ethnic discord, immigration policy, family values, mental health, and so forth? The striking characteristic of this theological trend is its recognition that social location is a factor in theological reflection affecting the critical questions theologians ask and the thought process they follow in addressing those questions as well as the answers that their theologies offer.

Critical questioning is as individual and as diverse as Christians and their situations. We ask questions not only of the specific prob-

> No question is off-limits to theological reflection. All questions are worth exploring. After all, if you do not ask, you will never know.

lem (who-what-where-when), but about how those elements relate to the core themes of our faith, applying the diagnostic tests of gospel, human condition, and Christian vocation (chaps. 5, 6, and 7).

No question is off-limits to theological reflection. All questions are worth exploring. After all, if you do not ask, you will never know. Whether a particular question is critical can really only be determined by asking it and seeing where it leads. If it helps to clarify our understanding of the meaning of faith, it has demonstrated its value.

Framing a View

Theologies identify the meaning of things viewed through the eyes of faith. These theological meanings are formed by acts of interpretation, correlation, and assessment. Remember Angelina and the theological view of her: she is "a child of God" (chap. 2). Her identity has been interpreted in light of the Christian message of God. This interpretation is correlated with other possible views: it is compatible with the view that she is the natural daughter of Gilbert and Teresa and incompatible with the view that she is "the Devil's seed." This interpretation is also value-assessed. As a child of God, she is precious to God. This assessment holds true even if it is later learned that Gilbert and Teresa had adopted her or if the whole world should turn against her and call her worthless. In one sense, then, theological reflection itself is the ongoing process of forming and re-forming such views.

There comes a time when we have to frame the view that is being formed. A photographer scans a field of vision through the

---

A theologian frames a particular view by selecting it amid the range of options and centering it within the crosshairs of the Christian faith and the life context.

---

viewfinder and frames the shot by fixing on one spot and bringing it into clear focus. A theologian also frames a particular view by selecting it amid the range of options and centering it within the crosshairs of the Christian faith and the life context. Using our embedded theology, we do this pretty much in simple "point-and-shoot" fashion. In deliberative theology, however, we adjust the aperture, zoom in or out, while double-checking whether we are getting the very best view possible. Careful observation of the scene and exploration of its relationship to the core concerns of faith can lead to a more intentional, refined understanding of what it means for our life and for the community of faith.

Once again, questioning is the primary means by which our view is brought into focus. Have I drawn appropriate resources from Scripture and tradition? Am I reasoning wisely? Does my own faith experience serve to sharpen or in some way obstruct my vision? What implications does my view of this matter have on my experience of faith and my understanding of that experience? For my situation and that of others? For my Christian calling? For the church? For my family and friends? For the world?

Judgment and Response

To judge, in the context of a critical theological method, is to make a choice. We select a view or an action that seems most apt in light of our deliberations. Most of the views we choose are subject to change as new information presents itself. Some of the actions we elect, like the decision to withdraw life support for Tom's mother, will be irrevocable; others, like the decision of an empty-nest mother to quit her job and volunteer at an AIDS hospice, are subject to adjustment and change.

It is tempting to do research and sort through data (observe and analyze) until kingdom come. But there is a reason why judgment, by whatever name, is a part of every critical method in every discipline. Critical thinking that stagnates at observation and analysis is self-indulgent.

We have to decide. Fear of being wrong is no excuse; it is a risk every theologian takes. With a critical method and the resources of Scripture and the church's tradition, experience, and reason to guide us, we reach a point where all of our deliberations bring us to a certain understanding or a sense that certain acts are more fitting than others. We form views, take a stand, commit ourselves, choose a course of action.

At this stage of theological reflection it is important to articulate reasons for our judgments and subsequent actions. Why is the decision to withdraw (or not withdraw) life support from Tom's mother the proper response of a family that is trying to be faithful to the gospel?

Explaining the rationale behind what we judge to be the appropriate Christian response to a particular issue is not just a formal

> Theological reflection occurs in the context of community. Because it is
> communal, it is also collaborative and dialogical.

exercise, done perhaps to satisfy a college or seminary professor. If
the community of faith is to be more than a cluster of individuals
espousing their individual theology ("This is what I believe; take it
or leave it"), then conversation must occur.

Indeed, theological reflection is insufficient if it is done in isolation. Theological reflection occurs in the context of community.
Because it is communal, it is also collaborative and dialogical. Even
though we eventually come up with our own unique operational
theology, its formation occurs in testing, sharing, talking, and listening to others.

Whether it happens at the local ministers' weekly breakfast,
while reading a recent book on liberation theology, under the
guidance of a spiritual director or pastoral supervisor, during dia-
logue and feedback with other members of the congregation, or in
intimate talks with friends and family members, theological reflection does not develop only from reviewing our private beliefs as
individuals or the writings of professional theologians. Our theology also is formed by the convictions of the community of faith.
We influence each other's understanding of the faith.

Theology is an individual task and a corporate enterprise.
Christians, as theologians, need to move beyond analysis and framing interpretations; we must make judgments and be prepared to
tell others why those judgments are warranted. Knowing why we
believe what we believe allows us to enter into conversation with
other Christians.

The community of faith is not only a community of worship
and fellowship; it is also one of critical deliberative theological
inquiry. We offer support to others, but we also offer them our
insights about the faith. We listen to theirs. Theological conversation occurs. We decide.

FOR FURTHER READING

Feldman, Edmund Burke. *Varieties of Visual Experience.* New York: Abrams, 1987. Feldman developed the definitive art-critical method upon which many other systems of critical thinking are based. This classic, lavishly illustrated book presents and applies the principles of criticism in a clear and understandable way.

Ottati, Douglas F. *Hopeful Realism: Reclaiming the Poetry of Theology.* Cleveland: Pilgrim Press, 1999. Ottati refers to the "poetry" of theology as the grand themes of the Christian faith (God, alpha and omega, Trinity, incarnation, sin and salvation, and others) whose meanings are far too grand to be reduced to mere slogans.

Stone, Karen. *Image and Spirit: How to Find Meaning in Visual Art.* Minneapolis: Augsburg, 2003. The author provides a theological and aesthetic background for a view of art as embodiment of the transcendent. Geared to the non-specialist, the book develops the reader's ability to interpret and appreciate artworks of any style or period from a spiritual perspective, offering specific tools of interpretation that use what is known about methods of critical thinking.

CHAPTER 9

FORMING SPIRIT

WAIT.

The first sight of a loved one who has been greatly changed by injury or illness often causes intense feelings of uneasiness, anxiety, or embarrassment. One woman, an artist, writes of this discomfort when she first saw her mother after a massive hemorrhagic stroke—hair shaved and head in a bonnet, skin yellow, left side slack, attached to feeding tubes, IVs, machines, shunt draining her brain of blood. "I told myself to wait, keep looking at her until I could get used to it. Just wait."[1] Her wait was rewarded with several joyful days of attending her mother's peaceful death.

Elsewhere she tells of the value of waiting when viewing an enigmatic, troubling, or disquieting piece of art: "Silence may be the act required . . . a kind of active passivity, an openness, a willingness to wait for the visible Word to disclose itself."[2]

As we fall silent
as we share another's vision
and make it ours
as we look and look and look
as we seek
we are apprehended.[3]

SPIRITUAL FORMATION

Listen. Attend. Wait. Receive. These are acts and attitudes of spiritual formation. They are also essential to our theological reflection.

In other chapters we made the point that a certain amount of distancing is necessary for doing theological reflection. Only by standing back from the particulars of our situation can we grow in understanding. We must take care, however, to avoid an attendant loss. The sensitive nature of an intimate relationship with God may be displaced by an attitude of detachment. Genuine concern for the meaning of our faith may give way to mere intellectualizing.

This intellectualizing is what some people outside of academic circles fear is all that career theological scholars do. Saying it isn't necessarily so does not make the fear go away. Theological scholarship often involves such enterprises as the painstaking examination of manuscript fragments, searching for the philosophical or social sources of a fifth-century creed, and making an inventory of various theological doctrines or psychological theories. Formal theological education itself is customarily split up into numerous specialized fields, such as biblical studies, dogmatic or systematic theology, history, ethics, pastoral care, religious education, and so forth. Each course has a particular slant. Each is offered by an expert who has studied in her

> If we lose touch with our base—our living sense of the love of God, the grace of Christ, and communion with the Holy Spirit—our efforts at theological reflection turn into make-work or a mere hobby.

or his subject area longer than the rest of us ever will, or even care to. Each supplies a piece of the puzzle necessary for assembling the overall picture of the gospel and ministry. It is easy for some, though, to become so caught up—or bogged down—in merely academic intricacies that the experiential roots of their faith go untended. Head without heart.

These roots deserve to be nurtured. If we lose touch with our base—our living sense of the love of God, the grace of Christ, and communion with the Holy Spirit—our efforts at theological reflection turn into make-work or a mere hobby. Their results become scattered and disjointed. Our "theology" sounds hollow.

So it is that theologians must tend the experiential roots of their faith. This is not to advocate that they merely turn inward, developing their personal relationship to God apart from friends, family, and church community or ignoring the tasks of working for reconciliation and justice in the world. It is to encourage them to make opportunities for refreshing their spirits, gathering things together in faith.

Spiritual formation is a traditional term, now in widespread use once again, for what we are describing. In the practice of spiritual disciplines such as worship, Scripture reading, meditation and prayer, or spiritual direction, we are not asleep or passive but *receptive,* sensitive to the presence of God and open to the power of the Spirit. We attend to the Word. Spiritual formation can enrich, balance, and inform our theological reflection, and bridge the gap between our experience and our study of faith.

Worship

Some modern Christians overlook corporate worship as a vital ingredient of their spiritual life. In corporate worship we involve our intellect, eyes, bodies, ears, the senses of touch and smell, even our sense of rhythm. We place ourselves in the presence of God but also in the company of other Christians. We find the means of grace proffered by the church, and we find our place in its history. We give ourselves the opportunity to consider those themes of faith and issues of the day around which we forge our theology.

Some denominations provide a theological explanation of the worship service that can be read on occasion (perhaps in lieu of the sermon) to help the congregation understand why they say and sing the words they do—what they mean theologically, and what they can mean for their daily lives. Often people are deeply moved when they come to understand the spiritual and emotional import of their worship.

There are many varieties of worship, each with its own richness, ranging from the quiet of a Friends meeting to the pageantry of High Mass in the Orthodox traditions. Every version brings Christians together in community. Every variation allows for spontaneity and free expression of the life of the community.

Every variation involves some repetition, follows certain patterns, develops traditions out of local preference and/or historical Christianity. Every variation fosters reflection on our faith.

It is a mistake to underestimate the spiritual potential of repetition. Your mind may drift, but each time you repeat the words and acts of worship they become a part of you. The late Karl Rolvaag, a former governor of Minnesota, once preached a sermon at a country church near his cabin in the north woods. He told of his personal spiritual journey and of his recovery first from alcoholism and then from a near-fatal automobile accident. The pastor of that country church traveled over two hundred miles to his hospital bed, where he lay injured and in a coma from his accident. She offered the service of Holy Communion. His lips began to move along with hers as she read the ancient words. He wept, he spoke, he raised his hand to receive the bread and wine. His rote repetition of those words and actions over the course of many years had implanted them in his being, and they broke through the barrier to consciousness when nothing else could. Theology became life.

Spiritual Disciplines

We operate each day in the presence of God. Through the centuries Christians have sought to deepen their awareness of that presence by tending to their spiritual lives.

Spirituality is not merely a matter of introspection nor of detached reflection, as some may think; it involves a relationship, a gift of grace. The giver determines that relationship, to be sure, but it also depends upon the recipient's active attention to the gift. (Here is the listening, the receptivity, we have referred to from the outset.) The disciplines of Scripture reading, meditation, and

> Spirituality is not merely a matter of introspection nor of detached reflection, as some may think; it involves a relationship, a gift of grace.

prayer remind us that our relationship with God is the overarching concern that focuses all others (while not negating or replacing them) and helps us rise beyond only basic human needs and desires to follow the gospel.

As Christians attend to their relationship with God, they are not necessarily on their own. Many churches provide devotional materials to aid people in their private spiritual disciplines. Historically the church has offered a practice known as *spiritual direction* to help heighten people's awareness of God's presence and to foster spiritual growth and formation. The spiritual director (clergy or lay) is a person whom Christians can visit and talk with specifically about that relationship. Each church tradition, and in individual cases the spiritual director, offers suggestions and specific methods for sensitizing people to God's presence and will—such as journaling, meditation, the *lectio divina* (a way to pray Scripture), or the imaging of portions of the Bible.

Paul distinguishes between the *nepioi,* those beginners in the faith who are fed only milk, and the *teleioi,* those more mature Christians who can receive solid food. It often seems many churches today focus so much on the *nepioi* that the *teleioi* are left to fend for themselves. They deliver many introductory lectures

> Spiritual formation is a bridge between theological reflection and day-to-day experience.

and not enough nourishment to help the faithful grow to a deeper understanding of the gospel and a more significant relationship with God. Whether from fear that something that is said will spark a controversy or concern that people will become bored, little is done in too many churches to help people reflect upon their embedded theology. Food for a mature faith, including elements for theological reflection, can be provided by the church's guidance in spiritual disciplines—whether under the leadership of spiritual directors, in sharing groups, or in educational settings.

Spiritual formation is a bridge between theological reflection and day-to-day experience. We return to the sources of faith. We focus on our relationship with God, the source of meaning and the giver of the power to live Christian lives faithful to the gospel in the community of faith.

A TRENCHES HERMENEUTIC

The process of theological reflection occurs in concrete life situations—perhaps in private spiritual crises, such as a struggle with dryness in one's devotional life, or in acts of Christian service, such as visiting an accident victim in the hospital, meeting with the worship committee, having coffee with a recently bereaved neighbor, or advocating for social justice.

Consider this hypothetical case: You stop at an antique flea market on the way home from work on a Friday evening. You are looking for turn-of-the-century mission oak furniture to replace the miscellaneous pieces that now grace your living room. After a quick run through the market, having found nothing of interest, you head back to your car. There on the ground next to your car is a man's wallet that has obviously fallen out of someone's pocket. Without a moment's hesitation you pick it up and get into your car. Opening the wallet you see that its owner lives only a few blocks from your home. You drive to the man's house and drop it off to a surprised but appreciative neighbor.

Why did you decide to return the wallet and the money in it? Without even weighing alternatives you made a choice. The action you took was a mere reflex; the decision posed no moral or theological dilemma. Yet, in fact, many things converged at that point. No doubt your decision was shaped in the distant past by values you learned or grew to hold important. Other people may have acted exactly as you did for reasons of their own. But your action was an outgrowth of your conviction that keeping something that was not rightfully yours would be an act of dishonesty and selfishness incompatible with your sense of Christian character. Your breeding in the faith formed an embedded theology that was heightened by your years in church school and later perhaps by deliberative theological reflection in the course of Bible study, discussion groups, or seminary education.

Your faith and values overrule certain responses at such times. If theological deliberation has already played a role in your faith development, the childhood lessons about honesty, unselfishness, and faithfulness have been examined from various sides. You know what you are and are not prepared to do, and under which circumstances. You will not keep the wallet even if you need the money or if its return inconveniences you. That conviction may seem obvious. (Would it be otherwise if your "social location" were not so secure and comfortable?) But because of previous thinking, other possibilities that might have a certain appeal are now overruled as well. You will not use the situation in order to teach the man to be more careful. You will not give the wallet to a charity, the church, or even a needy person you pass on the street.

To act in accordance with our Christian commitments, often there will not be the luxury of extended theological consideration. The theological work has to be done in advance—deliberative

> Christians need a foundation of prior deliberative theological reflection to prepare us as best as possible for dozens of daily choices as well as the life-altering decisions we face.

theological reflection—so that its results can inform our every choice. Major crises and momentous decisions, to be sure, will call for soul-searching before we find a remedy or choose a course of action. But even in those cases, such as Tom's crisis with his dying mother, our embedded theology may leave us ill prepared for the daunting task. Just as soldiers in the trenches have trained and practiced for the battle conditions they will encounter, we as Christians need a foundation of prior deliberative theological reflection to prepare us as best as possible for dozens of daily choices as well as the life-altering decisions we face.

Christian theologians must develop a way to internalize their theological reflection. It must be so simple that it can be acted upon at the spur of the moment, almost automatically; yet it must be so sophisticated that it can adapt to the complexities of the modern world. No single way is the correct one for everyone. Nevertheless, we believe that developing basic clarity on the issues raised by the three diagnostic exercises (gospel, the human condition, and vocation) will stand the Christian in good stead when facing the myriad of difficult situations that every day presents.

In some situations we may indeed have time to think, have conversation with other Christians, and devise appropriate responses. Within reason, for example, we can consider at length a plan for addressing needed emergency housing for women being battered by their husbands. But in other situations we may have to act reflexively, in a way that is comparable to the "muscle memory" we employ while driving a car. At such times we must trust that the Word resides within us, that the Christian faith is so ingrained in our living as to affect our decisions even when we do not have time to think them through, and that our theology is sufficiently deliberative to be faithful to its sources.

No theology is so well worked out that it is perfect and valid for every situation. We must continually make judgments and act upon them. These judgments and acts remain our frail attempts at truth. They are necessarily tentative; they must remain open to new input, to critique, to correction from the community, and to fresh insight.

Nevertheless, pursuing truth to the best of our ability, we need to make real commitments. Since at the point of action there is

> We need a theology that prepares us for the difficult business of being Christian in the fray of the real world, undergirds our commitment, and guides our action.

seldom enough time to go through a complicated procedure of theological reflection, we need an informed yet intuitive approach to the pastoral task and to Christian living—in short, a "trenches hermeneutic." We need a theology that prepares us for the difficult business of being Christian in the fray of the real world, undergirds our commitment, and guides our action.

One thing is certain: our prior reflection on theology and ministry *will* inform our practice. If we are attentive to the Word, the Christian faith will have its impact on what we do. As Christians and therefore theologians, we are called to listen and question, to forge an ever-growing understanding of the meaning of the Christian message of God, and to act on it in our lives, in the church, and in the world.

FOR FURTHER READING

Bidwell, Duane. *Short-term Spiritual Guidance*. Creative Pastoral Care and Counseling series. Minneapolis: Fortress Press, 2004. Bidwell develops from the fields of brief therapy and spiritual direction a very practical way people can listen to God's presence and respond to it.

Conroy, Maureen. *The Discerning Heart: Discovering a Personal God*. Chicago: Loyola Press, 1993. A thorough and accessible introduction to spiritual discernment, *The Discerning Heart* includes exercises and practical questions to help the reader develop the ability of discernment of God's presence.

Maas, Robin, and Gabriel O'Donnell. *Spiritual Traditions for the Contemporary Church*. Nashville: Abingdon Press, 1990. Maas and O'Donnell offer a serious discussion of historical and ecumenically diverse traditions of spirituality, including "the feminine dimension(s) in Christian Spirituality." Included are suggestions for readers interested in engaging in any of the various practices discussed.

Mursell, Gordon. *The Story of Christian Spirituality*. Minneapolis: Fortress Press; Oxford: Lion Publishing, 2001. This is a sound, informative survey of the ongoing Christian concern for spirituality.

GLOSSARY

Anthropological starting point. Human starting point; a procedure by which theologians reflect first on Christian faith in the context of human living and then move to ascertain the meaning of God's message to the world as set forth in Scripture and/or tradition.

Anthropology. The study and doctrine of the human being; *theological* anthropology typically focuses on the nature, possibilities, limits, and ultimate destiny of humanity in relationship to God.

Bilateral cognition. The process of organizing information by means of parallel synthetic thinking and sequential thinking in concert.

Canon. Literally, a "reed" used as measuring rod; hence a rule, standard, or official list. The Christian biblical canon is the collection of writings deemed sacred, incomparable, and authoritative testimony of God's message to the world.

Canonical force. The influence, both formative and constraining, that the biblical canon as a literary whole of many parts exerts on the life and thought of Christians because of its distinctive status, arrangement, and contents.

Christian appropriateness. Concern for the "Christianness" of a theology, that is, its rootage in, compatibility with, and faithfulness to the Christian message.

Christology. The study and doctrine of Jesus Christ, customarily focusing on both the person (the nature and status) and the saving work of Christ.

Church. The community (assembly, congregation, body) of the faithful called forth by God for worship, proclamation of the gospel, and service to the world in the name of Jesus Christ.

Conscientiousness. From *conscience,* the capacity to identify and conform to standards of what is good and right; here, conscientiousness is an intense concern to be, to say, and to do only that which is in keeping with a sense of the fear and love of the will of God.

Correlation. The process of bringing two or more discrete entities into mutual relation; here, investigation of similarities and differences between the meaning of things as viewed in light of Christian faith and as viewed from other standpoints.

Creeds, confessions of faith. Summary declarations regarding matters of faith in which Christians devoutly believe and commit to uphold in their teachings and practices. They often serve as official touchstones of community identity. Affirmations, articles, declarations, and fundamentals of faith are among the terms frequently used in churches as equivalent to creed or confession.

Critical inquiry. An investigation that, seeking to take nothing for granted, proceeds by asking questions; in modern theology, critical inquiry has dealt especially with questions about the meaning of faith in light of reason (philosophy, science, and experience), the study of history, and social-scientific considerations (for instance, sociological, psychological, political, and economic issues).

Deliberative theology. Here, a process of reflecting on multiple understandings of the faith implicit in the life and witness of Christians in order to identify and/or develop the most adequate understanding possible.

Doctrine(s). Literally, teaching(s); the whole body of Christian teaching regarding the meaning of faith, customarily divided into that which is to be believed (Christian doctrine in the narrow sense) and that which is to be done (moral doctrine or ethics).

Ecclesiology. The study and doctrine of the Christian church, customarily focusing on the distinctive identity, nature, and purpose of the community of faith.

Ecumenical movement. Also *ecumenism*. The quest to overcome divisions among Christians and their diverse churches in order to promote the worldwide unity of the church.

Eisegesis. A derogatory term for the practice of imposing one's own ideas on Scripture rather than drawing out the meaning of the texts by careful, thoroughgoing study.

Embedded theology. Here, the understanding(s) of faith disseminated by the church and assimilated by its members in their daily lives.

Eschatology. The study and doctrine of last or final things, focusing usually on what is to happen when God's purposes for creation are fully realized at the end of human history.

Exegesis. The analysis and explanation of the meaning of Scripture drawn from close, careful, thoroughgoing study of the texts.

Extra ecclesiam nulla salus est. Literally, "outside the church, there is no salvation." The view that salvation is possible only for those belonging to the Christian community of faith.

Faith. The response and commitment to the message of God; here, a comprehensive term for the elements of the Christian life, including heartfelt devotion to God, belief, and obedient action.

Gospel. Literally, "good news" or "glad tidings." In Christian theology, the gospel is the good news to the world regarding what God has done in Jesus Christ; hence the term was given to the biblical writings (that is, Matthew, Mark, Luke, and John) focusing on "the story" of Jesus.

Grace. A gift that is bestowed by God; in Christian accounts of salvation, especially, the gift of God's merciful forgiveness and loving acceptance of human beings despite their sin.

Hermeneutics. The study and theory of interpretation; biblical hermeneutics focuses on approaches, principles, and guidelines for the interpretation of Scripture.

Intelligibility. Concern for the clarity, coherence, and understandability of a Christian theology.

Justification. God's merciful declaration (verdict) of acceptance of sinners in Jesus Christ.

Kerygma. Literally, "preaching" or "proclamation"; a concise declaration of the central content of God's message of salvation in Jesus Christ.

Law. The obligations (commandments) that set forth God's will regarding what humans are to be, to say, and to do.

Mariology. Especially in Roman Catholic theology, the study and doctrine of Mary, the mother of Jesus Christ.

Means of grace. Specific, finite actions (especially, preaching and the sacraments) by which the gospel is proclaimed and its benefits appropriated by the faithful.

Ministry. Literally, "service"; the service(s)—worship, proclamation of the gospel, care for others—that God calls Christians to undertake in faithful response to the gospel.

Mission. Literally, "sending forth"; the task(s) which the church and its members are sent out by God into the world to perform.

Moral absolutes; moral absolutism. The view that certain rules for living have been established (by God, in Christianity) as unalterably fixed for every person, time, and circumstance.

Moral integrity. Here, concern for the ethical standards implicit or explicit in any given theology.

Norma normans sed non normata. Literally, "a norm which norms but is not normed." A Protestant phrase highlighting the Bible as the incomparable standard for theology.

Orthodoxy. Correct ("right") opinion; often, concern for firm assent and strict adherence to a church's teaching regarding the basic truths of faith.

Orthopraxy. Correct ("right") action and practice; often, concern for the unwavering, scrupulous observance of certain practices and/or the fulfillment of certain duties.

Parallel synthetic thinking. Thinking that processes information all at once as a totality (a *Gestalt*) without separately examining each of the interrelated components.

Plausible coherence. Concern to set forth the multifaceted meaning of Christian faith as an interrelated whole that, while not internally contradictory, eludes fixture in a seamless web of strict logical consistency.

Pneumatology. The study and doctrine of the Holy Spirit.

Proof-texting. The practice of picking and choosing portions of the Scripture to support a particular (pre-chosen) view.

Revelatory starting point. A procedure in which theologians focus first on the message of God as set forth in Scripture and/or tradition and then move on to ascertain its implications for humanity and human life.

Sacrament(s). A visible (material) sign of the invisible (spiritual) grace of God by which the gospel is proclaimed and its benefits are appropriated by the faithful. Seven such signs—with words and actions and/or elements—became established in the Roman Catholic and Orthodox churches: baptism, eucharist (the Lord's Supper), confirmation, penance, marriage, holy orders, and anointing of the sick. Protestants typically designate only the first two of these as sacraments.

Salvation. The gift of God that heals (redeems, releases, restores, liberates) human beings from sin and sinfulness and brings them to the life that the goodness and mercy of God proposes for them. Often spoken of as though it applies only to individuals, salvation is also used as a comprehensive term for the full realization of the purposes of God—that God's will be done on earth as in heaven—with the establishment of peace, justice, and joy and the renewing and/or restoration of the whole of creation.

Sanctification. The working out, as aided by the power of the Spirit, of a life of truly faithful services of love and obedience to God's will in thankfulness for the gospel.

Scripture(s). The Bible; the Christian biblical canon that includes the sacred literature of the people of Israel (the Hebrew Scriptures or Old Testament), and the literature of early Christianity (the New Testament).

Sequential thinking. Processing information in a linear, step-by-step fashion.

Sin(s). Specific words, deeds, thoughts, or desires in violation of or disobedience to God's will.

Sinfulness. The state or condition of being at odds with God's will, which accounts for and/or leads to specific sin(s).

Sola scriptura. Literally, "the Scripture alone"; a Protestant phrase signaling a commitment to develop and test Christian living (including the church and its theology) solely on the basis of the authority of the Bible.

Soteriology. The study and doctrine of salvation.

Spirituality; spiritual practices and disciplines. In Christian theology, the experience of a profound relationship of intimacy with God, Jesus Christ, and the Spirit. In Reformation and post-Reformation times, Protestants typically substituted for the traditional Catholic term *spirituality* other words like *piety* or *godliness*.

Template. A pattern (network) of categories used to sort and organize information into a manageable whole.

Theodicy. The attempt to explain how the power and goodness of God can be reconciled with the experience of evil.

Theological analysis. The investigative side of theology that seeks to sort out and evaluate the understanding of faith implicit or explicit in any given statement and/or action.

Theological construction. The synthetic (integrative) side of theology that seeks to fashion a fresh exposition of the meaning of faith in the Christian message.

Theological method. The procedure followed in the process of theological reflection. Also, the study of the sources, the ordering of topics and materials, and the criteria for evaluating a theology.

Theological reflection (Christian). The process of thinking about the meaning of faith in the Christian message of God.

Theology. Literally, a statement or account (*logos*) about God (*theos*); also, the study and doctrine of God. A comprehensive term for the various studies of matters relating to faith, church, and ministry. Here, broadly and in keeping with the view of theology as "faith seeking understanding," theology is the process of thinking about, developing, and stating (in words and/or actions) an understanding of the meaning of faith in the Christian message of God.

Tradition; traditions. The activity of transmitting (handing down, passing along) the meaning of faith from one person or generation to another; it also refers to the sum total of that which is available for transmission by this means. The term *traditions* can refer to specific items that a given Christian community transmits to others in that community as the meaning of faith and faithfulness.

Validity. A concern for the reliability, reality, and truth(fulness) of theological views.

Vocation. Literally, "calling"; the summons that God issues to the faithful to live lives of devotion, obedience, and service.

Word of God. The self-disclosure of God coming as a message (a speaking, an address) to the world.

NOTES

Introduction

1. Once commonplace, the notion of theology as a craft has been revived in recent years: see, for instance, Avery Dulles, *The Craft of Theology: From Symbols to System*, New Expanded Edition (New York: Herder & Herder, 1995); Charles Wood, *Vision and Discernment: An Orientation in Theological Study* (Atlanta: Scholars Press, 1985). See also Patricia O'Connell Killen and John de Beer, *The Art of Theological Reflection* (New York: Crossroad, 1994); Evelyn Eaton Whitehead and James Whitehead, *Method in Ministry*, Revised Edition (Chicago: Sheed and Ward, 1995).

3. Resources for Theological Reflection

1. Gerhard Ebeling, "Church History Is the History of the Exposition of Scripture," in *The Word of God and Tradition*, trans. S. H. Hooke (Philadelphia: Fortress Press, 1968), 11–31.

2. David Kelsey, *Proving Doctrine: Uses of Scripture in Recent Theology* (Harrisburg, Pa.: Trinity Press International, 1999).

4. Theological Method

1. See Graham Wallas, *The Art of Thought* (London: Butler & Tanner, 1926).

6. The Human Condition

1. See, e.g., "The Twelve Articles of the Upper Swabian Peasants," in *The Radical Reformation*, ed. and trans. Michael G. Baylor (Cambridge: Cambridge University Press, 1991), 231–38.

9. Forming Spirit

1. Karen Stone, "Underneath Are the Everlasting Arms," in *Reflections on Grief and Spiritual Growth* (Nashville: Abingdon Press, 2005), 140.

2. Ibid., 58.

3. Ibid., 142. Used by permission of the author.

INDEX

Abortion, 15, 117
Adequacy. *See* Assessment
African American religion, 5, 8, 55
Angelou, Maya, 84
Anthropology
    doctrine, 29, 85
    starting point, 60–61
Aristotle, 85
Assessment, theological, 27, 35–40,
    100–107, 114–20

Baptism, 33, 37
Belief, 9
Bible
    biblical studies, 5, 49
    relation to theology, 46–50
    as Scripture, 46–50, 54, 73, 75–
    77, 127
Brant, C. H., 54

Canon, 46–50
Christian
    identity, 7, 8, 12, 33, 74, 99–102
    message. *See* Revelation
    tradition, 50–52
Christians, ordinary, 1–4, 6, 13–14,
    15–16, 18–19, 20–21
Church communities, 9, 13, 21–23,
    55, 75–76, 89, 99, 101–2,
    108–10, 125
Correlation, 27, 30–35, 44, 56, 118
Craft, theological, 2, 27–28, 66, 113
Creation, 33
Creeds, 20, 51

Deliberative theology, 16–21, 22–24,
    42, 52, 75, 114–20
Decisions, 19, 101–8

Doctrines, 8, 20, 29, 51

Ebeling, Gerhard, 46
Ecclesiology. *See* Church
    communities
Embedded theology, 13–16, 18, 20,
    28, 39, 65, 105, 115, 127, 128,
    129
Ethics. *See* Morality
Euripides, 84
Euthanasia, 63, 108
Exegesis, 49. *See also* Interpretation
Experience, 20–21, 53–56

Faith, 7, 10, 11–12, 14, 29–30, 44,
    52–53, 60–61, 77

God, 7, 14, 21, 35, 54, 55, 64, 73, 74,
    83, 88, 125–27
Gospel, 7, 50, 72–78. *See also*
    Revelation
Grace, 88–89, 94, 126

Hermeneutics, 28–30, 49–50, 128–30
Hitler, Adolf, 107
Homelessness, 104–5, 107–12
Human condition, 68, 83–90. *See
    also* Anthropology
Hymnal example, 62, 63–64, 67, 71,
    76, 104, 115

Iconoclast controversy, 106
Interpretation in theology, 8, 27,
    28–30, 31, 49, 50

Jesus Christ, 7, 73, 74, 75, 77–78, 89

Kelsey, David, 48–49